Temperament in the Classroom

Temperament in the Classroom

Understanding Individual Differences

by

Barbara K. Keogh, Ph.D.
University of California,
Los Angeles

·P·A·U·L·H·
BROOKES
PUBLISHING CO.®

Baltimore • London • Sydney

Paul H. Brookes Publishing Co.
Post Office Box 10624
Baltimore, Maryland 21285-0624

www.brookespublishing.com

Typeset by Barton Matheson Willse & Worthington,
Baltimore, Maryland.
Manufactured in the United States of America
by Versa Press, East Peoria, Illinois.

Individuals described herein are composites or fictional
accounts based on actual experiences. Individuals' names
have been changed, and identifying details have been altered
to protect confidentiality.

Library of Congress Cataloging-in-Publication Data

Keogh, Barbara K.
    Temperament in the classroom : understanding individual differences /
    by Barbara K. Keogh.
        p.   cm.
    Includes bibliographical references and index.
    ISBN 1-55766-601-6
    1. Learning, Psychology of.   2. Temperament in children.   3. Child
    development.   I. Title.

LB1060 .K46 2003
370.15'23—dc21

                                                                2002035639

British Library Cataloguing in Publication data are available
from the British Library.

Contents

About the Author vii

Foreword
Stella Chess, M.D., with *Alexander Thomas, M.D.* ix

Preface xiii

Acknowledgments xvii

Chapter 1
Temperament in the Classroom:
    An Overview 1

Chapter 2
What Is Temperament? 11

Chapter 3
Why Understanding Temperament Is Important 27

Chapter 4
What Is the Basis of Temperament? .47

Chapter 5
Does Temperament Influence Children's
    Achievement in School? 61

Chapter 6
Does Temperament Influence Teachers' Academic
    Decisions? . . . . . : 77

Chapter 7
Are Temperament and Behavior Problems
    Related? 93

Chapter 8
Temperament and Children with Disabilities 109

Chapter 9
How Is Temperament Assessed? 125

Chapter 10
How Can Temperament Knowledge Be Applied
    in School? 141

Bibliography
        References 163
        Recommended Readings 174

Appendices
    Appendix A: Longitudinal Studies of
    Temperament 179
    Appendix B: Scales and Questionnaires for
    Assessing Temperament 183
    Appendix C: Publications and Programs
    on Temperament for Teachers and
    Parents 187

Index 193

About the
Author

Barbara K. Keogh, Ph.D., is a professor in the University of California, Los Angeles (UCLA), Department of Psychiatry and a licensed clinical psychologist. Dr. Keogh has experience in school, juvenile court, and medical/psychiatric settings. She was a professor in the Graduate School of Education at UCLA for 25 years.

Dr. Keogh has been an active member of many organizations serving adults and children with disabilities, including the National Advisory Committee on the Handicapped. She continues to serve as a consultant to a number of governmental and private agencies including the U.S. Department of State Office of Overseas Schools and the National Center for Learning Disabilities. She received the 1992 Research Award from the Council for Exceptional Children and the 1997 Professional Contribution Award from the Learning Disabilities Association of America.

Dr. Keogh has authored or co-authored a number of books and many articles focused on temperament and on children with learning and developmental challenges, including *Research on Classroom Ecologies* (co-authored with Speece, Lawrence Erlbaum

Associates, 1996) and *Research and Global Perspectives in Learning Disabilities* (co-authored with Hallahan, Lawrence Erlbaum Associates, 2001). She received her bachelor of arts degree from Pomona College, her master's degree from Stanford University, and her doctorate degree from the Claremont Graduate School, all in psychology.

Foreword

It is my genuine pleasure to write this Foreword to *Temperament in the Classroom: Understanding Individual Differences.* This is a particularly fortunate period for such a volume to appear, for the need is great. There is a swell of concern in our national educational system lest it be failing to provide adequate basic education as well as preparing students for higher education. The 21st century has ushered in an expanding interest on the part played by children's temperament in their educational development. Dr. Keogh is well known for examining and reporting on the complexities of classroom atmosphere, the strengths and weaknesses the pupils bring to the educational process, and educators' curricular expectations in a way that is always crystal clear and jargon-free. Her work has centered on the fascinating fugue of interplay in the classroom. This dance includes the ways in which individual behavioral styles (temperament) of children and the individual teaching styles of teachers influence each other. Most important to this book are the examples of goodness or poorness of fit; in other words, how school-room atmosphere and teacher's expectations and temperaments match children's intellectual abilities, temperaments, individual talents, and expectations.

The organization of chapters is highly useful. Starting with a definition of temperament, the book moves into discussions of why an understanding of temperament is important in the school environment, how it influences teachers' educational decisions, and how it is an important factor in behavior problems in the classroom. A most important chapter reports on the influence of temperament in children with disabilities. Specifically recommended in this book is the discussion on restless and active children in the classroom as distinguished from children with diagnosed attention-deficit/hyperactivity disorder.

My appreciation of Dr. Keogh's book is enhanced by my own childhood memories of my mother's classroom tales. She had been a grade school teacher who was dedicated to her pupils' learning success. One such student was Mary, a shy 7-year-old. Because Mary exhibited discomfort when asked to respond aloud, her first-grade teacher had ceased to call on her. Mary entered my mother's second-grade class a virtual non-reader, though her schoolwork and homework showed that she was good in math. Assuming that Mary's potential was there, my mother began tutoring the child before school, at recess, and after school when there were no inhibiting onlookers. When it was evident that progress was occurring, she drilled Mary 2 weeks ahead on a passage that the students were to read aloud in class; this practice became a conspiracy between the two. In the reading lesson, she called on Mary in a casual manner, and to the classmates' surprise, Mary read the passage faultlessly. My mother told her colleagues that she introduced Mary as "a participating scholar" and boosted her self-confidence. When the going had been hard, my mother bribed Mary with pennies or candies (now called "token economies"). Then the crowning step was for Mary to tell her mother, Mrs. T. that her teacher wanted to see her before school the next morning. When Mrs. T. arrived, my mother said, "You think that Mary cannot read. I want to show you what an excellent reader she is." Mary then read the memorized passage out loud, which was followed by her mother's fulsome praise of her daughter's intelligence and perseverance. This provided another boost to Mary's self-respect.

Another example from my mother's teaching career was the story of Burt, an 8-year-old in my mother's third-grade class who had worn out his second-grade teacher with his boundless energy. My mother saw nothing unusual about Burt's behavior—she herself had grown up with four younger brothers. Good natured as Burt was, however, his wriggling and wanderings around the room did not make for a good teaching atmosphere. My mother saw this as her problem to solve. When Burt began to be restless, my mother suddenly found errands that she needed done and asked Burt to help. Papers needed to be passed out, which required that Burt go to each desk; classroom books needed to be rearranged; the blackboard needed erasing. When Burt again began to appear distracted, my mother used her "ace." She sent a very important message to another teacher whose room was located at the far end of the corridor. The note she sent said, "I just needed to get Burt's muscles in motion. Please send me a sealed note back and thank him for doing such an important job." This device helped Burt stay focused until the lunch break. No medication was used; indeed, none was available. No scolding, no put downs, and no build up of oppositional behavior or resentment on either side was necessary. And again, there was no thought on my mother's part that she had done anything unusual. She was simply being a good teacher and assisting a restless child to become educated!

What was so impressive to me, as I reflected on these stories as a practicing child and adolescent psychiatrist trying to devise strategies for collaboration with schools, was that my mother and her friends did not think they were doing anything very special. They were simply doing their jobs, increasing their teaching skills, and gaining immense satisfaction. What's more, they were considering each child's temperament and including this understanding of temperament in their instructional and management practices.

Rethinking *Temperament in the Classroom: Understanding Individual Differences* in the light of my teacher-mother's perspectives, I am even more convinced of how helpful this book is for both new and experienced teachers and other educators, and how enlightening for parents.

Stella Chess, M.D.
Professor of Child Psychiatry

with

Alexander Thomas, M.D.
Professor of Psychiatry

New York University Medical Center

Preface

This book is about temperament in the context of schools and classrooms. Over the years I have become increasingly aware of the ways individual differences in temperament affect how children experience their worlds, including how they build and conduct their relationships with both adults and peers. My interest in temperament is based partly on my experience with my own children, who differed in their temperamental characteristics despite having the same parents and at least similar home environments. My interest was reinforced by my experience as a clinical psychologist and then as a school psychologist, positions that gave me opportunities to observe children and teachers at work in the classroom and on the playground. As a professor at the University of California, Los Angeles, I was able to study systematically the impact of temperament in families and in schools for more than two decades.

The journey to writing this book has been a long and rather circuitous one. My academic training was as a developmental psychologist but I have always been interested in how psychology could be applied to education. Often the two disciplines follow separate paths with relatively little meaningful interchange. I have been fortunate to have worked in both disciplines and see many ways in which each informs the other. Certainly both have added to my thinking about children and school; my ideas are based on my own research and clinical experiences as well as the research of others.

While living in England for a year during my husband's sabbatical leave from UCLA, I studied how children responded to a task in which they were asked to copy two- and three-dimensional designs. All of the children, although of different ages, could solve the tasks, but their attitudes and strategies were strikingly different. Some were timid, shy, and hesitant; others were immediately involved and enthusiastic; some were reflective and persistent; others were impulsive and distracted. Many children used verbal cues, but others "practiced" the designs by drawing in the air; some broke down the designs into parts and relied on analytic step-by-step solutions, while others approached the designs as if they were all one piece. All of the children completed the designs, but their behavioral styles differed widely.

Back in the United States, a more clinical experience added to my awareness of how temperament contributed to children's adjustment in school. A preschool in the UCLA Department of Pediatrics provided services to children with disabilities and served as a training facility for UCLA students. The children's disabilities ranged in type and severity and the program provided many opportunities for peer interactions and socialization. One of students with the most severe physical limitations was a 4-year-old boy with cerebral palsy who had no speech and only minimal locomotion. Yet he was a magnet for the other children and the staff. He was an exceptionally responsive, cheerful, and outgoing child who thrived on interactions with others and who, despite serious physical limitations, was the most popular child in the class. Other children with milder disabilities were less sought after and had fewer and less satisfactory personal relationships. The differences in these children's temperaments were striking.

In a large research effort directed at early identification of children "at risk" for low achievement in school, a team of graduate students and I worked in four kindergarten classes in a large elementary school in southern California. We assessed the children with a range of measures and observed behavior in the classroom. The range of temperaments of the children in the different classrooms was very similar; however, one of the four classes had an extraordinarily high number of children considered at risk because of their behavior and achievement (despite assurances from the principal that the children had been randomly assigned to classrooms). Based on these findings we realized how important it was to consider the characteristics of children relative to characteristics in the classroom. Thus, a basic theme in this book is how individual differences in children's temperaments and the context of classrooms contribute to children's experiences and achievement in school.

I have learned a great deal in this venture, and I am now even more convinced of how important an understanding of temperament is in schools. I hope that teachers and other school professionals will find the content useful in working with the many different children who fill school classrooms every day.

Acknowledgments

I have found while writing this book that it is not possible to do it alone; I have been helped by a number of people. I thank Carol Lindsay of North Idaho College; Robin Holmes of the Boise, Idaho, Schools; and Cindy Bernheimer at University of California, Los Angeles, for slogging through drafts of the chapters and for their careful reviews and suggestions. I also thank Ronald Gallimore at UCLA for computer help in preparing this manuscript. I thank especially my husband, Jack Keogh, for his interest and encouragement, for long dinner table discussions, and for taking on the very tedious task of reference checking. This book would not have been finished without the help of all of these people. I cannot thank them enough. I have also been fortunate to have friendships with temperament pioneers Stella Chess and Alexander Thomas, pediatrician William Carey, and psychologist Roy Martin; their insights have added immeasurably to my understanding of temperament and schooling.

To Jack, Kirk, Carol, and Bruce

In memory of Kelly

CHAPTER 1

Temperament in the Classroom
An Overview

Each fall the process begins anew. Hundreds of thousands of pupils and tens of thousands of teachers begin the annual migration to the classroom. The pupils are many ages and sizes. They come from different ethnic, cultural, and linguistic backgrounds. Some have the aptitudes and experiences necessary for success in school. Others have limited skills or have not had opportunities to master the prerequisite knowledge demanded in the classroom. Some come to school eagerly—motivated to learn and confident that they will be successful. Others approach school reluctantly—uncertain about themselves and about the academic and social demands of school.

Teachers, too, are of many ages and different ethnic, cultural, and linguistic backgrounds. Like pupils, they approach the start of school differently. Some are experienced and well prepared. Others are novices, facing a classroom of students for the first time. Some are confident; some are fearful. Some are enthusiastic; others dread the start of the school year.

Both pupils and teachers bring a range of individual differences to school, yet the expectation is that they share a common goal of acquiring new knowledge and skills. They will spend 5 days a week together in the same classroom for 8 or 9 months. For some, this will be a positive experience, but for others the months will be filled with stress and unhappiness. The students will not have learned and the teachers will feel dissatisfied and unsuccessful.

What accounts for these differences in experiences? Certainly the physical conditions of classrooms and schools and the resources available affect learning. Some aspects of school life are very basic or tangible. Do students feel safe? Are text books and instructional materials available? Is the classroom overcrowded? Have teachers been well prepared in the subject matter to be taught and for the many demands of the classroom?

Other contributing factors to successful schooling, not as overt, lie in the students themselves. Many student characteristics contribute to whether the students' experiences in school are positive or negative and to whether they are learning or simply passing time. Students differ in academic aptitudes, in cognitive abilities, in linguistic skills, even in the languages they speak. In addition to their previous learning opportunities and experiences, students' attitudes, motivations, and interests affect how they respond to the content and the methods of instruction. They also affect how students interact with teachers and with peers. Similarly, teachers' knowledge and abilities, their instructional skills, their interests, their expectations, and their motivations influence how they organize and manage the classroom, how they teach, and how they interact with students.

Differences in knowledge, aptitude, motivation, cultural background, and interests alone neither explain nor capture fully the nature of children's and teachers' experiences in school, however. Classroom life is also affected by individual differences in temperament. Indeed, students' and teachers' temperaments have powerful interactive effects that contribute to their experiences in school. These interactions are the focus of this book.

WHAT IS TEMPERAMENT?

Temperament is one of those elusive and hard-to-define characteristics that describe individual differences among people. Researchers classify specific temperaments differently, but on a day-to-day basis, parents and teachers have a "we know it when we see it" attitude. All of us recognize individuals who have a slow tempo; they move through life at an unhurried pace, are slow to respond, and are slow to action. In the classroom, these students often have trouble finishing assignments; they lag behind their peers, and they are constantly playing "catch up" with others. We also know highly active, impulsive, quick-to-respond people who go through life at high speed. As children, they are the students who start to work on an assignment before the teacher has finished the instructions and rush to get to the end of a book or a project. Some children find any change in routine upsetting; they take time to adjust to new situations, new seating arrangements, new classroom routines, and new people. In contrast, we know other children who thrive on novelty, who seek out new experiences, and who interact vigorously with teachers and classmates. These personal characteristics reflect individual differences in temperament.

Temperament differs from other individual attributes such as intelligence, motivation, or interests. Those describe what people *do* and why and how well they do it. Temperament refers to *how* they do it. We often hear children described as bright; hard working; or interested in sports, card collecting, or music. These descriptors refer to the content of what children do and how interested they are to do it, but they do not address temperamental differences or behavioral styles that characterize individuals. To get a picture of children's temperament or behavioral style, think of how differently students respond when a teacher gives a new assignment, how they differ in persistence when faced with a long project, or how quickly or slowly they settle down after returning from recess.

Temperament as Behavioral Style

The definition of temperament proposed by psychiatrists Thomas and Chess specifically captured the notion of behavioral style. They defined temperament ". . . as a general term referring to the *how* of behavior. It differs from ability, which is concerned with the *what* and *how well* of behaving, and from motivation that accounts for *why* a person does what he is doing" (1977, p. 9).

Temperamental differences are apparent in many situations, including schools and classrooms. Almost all children go to school, yet their responses to the first days of school vary widely. Compared with children who enter school enthusiastically, shy children tend to stand back on the sidelines and watch until they feel comfortable and at ease, for example.

Differences in temperament or behavioral styles may have positive or negative effects on children's experiences in the classroom. Teachers will recognize elementary school children who respond quickly and intensely to others around them and who are distracted by the many ongoing activities in the classroom. They will also recognize those active, energetic children who respond eagerly to new experiences and novelty, as well as those children who withdraw from new demands and situations and who may be reluctant learners. Such individual differences in behav-

Raoul and Stevie, both 5 years old, are entering the classroom on the first day of kindergarten. Both are with their mothers. Raoul immediately leaves his mother's side and makes a beeline for the tank filled with colorful tropical fish. He is soon in conversation with several other children, and he and this little group rush off to explore the playhouse and playground equipment. Stevie remains by his mother near the doorway. He watches the other children but makes no move to join them. After 10 to 15 minutes of quiet observation, he moves to the fish tank and tentatively begins to interact with several other children. As the day goes on, both boys become involved and active, but their initial responses to this new situation and the time they took to adapt were very different.

ioral styles are important influences on how children experience school.

The recognition that there are individual differences in temperament is not new; rather, they have long been noted. The early Greeks described individuals as phlegmatic, choleric, melancholic, and sanguine—personal styles the Greeks associated with four body humors. Sheldon (1942) proposed three body types—ectomorph, mesomorph, and endomorph—and linked each to a different temperament. Novelists and playwrights have described their heroes and heroines in temperament terms, such as Shakespeare's Hamlet, the "melancholy Dane"; the dour Mr. Rochester in Charlotte Bronte's *Jane Eyre;* the responsible Beezus and her spunky and mischievous sister Ramona Quimby in Beverly Cleary's *Beezus and Ramona;* or the amiable Winnie the Pooh in A.A. Milne's famous children's stories.

Children's behavior and development are obviously affected by environmental conditions, but those conditions do not operate on a *tabula rasa,* or blank slate. Rather, children bring unique intellectual aptitudes, physical abilities, and language skills to school. They also bring differences in temperament. These personal differences affect how individual children respond to the school environment and how they interact with teachers and peers. Thus, these personal differences have consequences for adjustment and achievement. A great deal of attention has been paid to the contribution of intellectual and language abilities to success in school, but relatively little has been directed at the role of temperament.

Stylistic attributes making up temperament are less amenable to quantitative assessment compared with cognitive ability or achievement in reading and arithmetic and, therefore, don't lend themselves easily to traditional research designs. Still, findings from many groundbreaking studies have contributed to the temperament dialogue. This book describes the research base documenting how temperament contributes to students' achievement, adjustment, and personal experience in school.

WHAT DO WE KNOW ABOUT TEMPERAMENT?

What is the research basis supporting the concept of temperament? More specifically, what do we know about temperament that is relevant to children's educational experiences? Temperament is a personal characteristic that has been studied from biological, neurological, and behavioral/psychological perspectives. Individual differences in children's temperaments have been linked to a number of developmental, personal, and educational outcomes. Psychiatrists, psychologists, pediatricians, and other clinicians who work with individual children and their families have found temperament to be an important and useful concept in understanding problems in children's development and adjustment. They have provided rich data describing behavior problems and approaches to treatment and interventions of clinical conditions. Developmental psychologists, behavioral geneticists, and educators have expanded our knowledge of temperament through research with groups of children using both cross-sectional and longitudinal methods. These researchers have helped define and describe different approaches to temperament and have provided information about the organization or structure of temperament characteristics as well as about the stability of temperament.

Longitudinal studies are of particular interest in that the same children are studied over time and in different developmental periods, thus providing information about stability and change and about long-term effects of temperament. Three examples of major longitudinal research projects are described here briefly and are referred to in a number of places in this book. (See Appendix A for more detailed descriptions.)

- *The New York Longitudinal Study* (NYLS; Thomas & Chess, 1977) was one of the first major studies of temperament. Begun in 1956, the study assessed 131 children as infants and at 3, 6, and 9 years of age using psychometric techniques, behavioral observations, and interviews with parents and teachers. Psychiatrists Thomas and Chess followed these children into adulthood; as of 2002, these individuals were in their fifties.

- *The Dunedin Longitudinal Study* began in 1972 in New Zealand (Silva, 1990). Information was gathered on more than 1,100 children in their first months of life, and beginning at age 3, the children were reassessed every 2 years using a range of psychological, medical, and sociological measures. More than 1,000 individuals in this study were reassessed at age 18.

- *The Australian Temperament Project* (Prior, Sanson, Smart, & Oberklaid, 2000) began in 1980 and initially studied 2,443 infants between the ages of 4–8 months. The children and their families were followed up at periods of approximately 18 months, and about 70% of the original sample was still enrolled in the study more than a decade later. Data collected during follow-ups included information about children's temperament, developmental status, and schooling.

These longitudinal studies were conducted in different countries, with different groups of children, and with somewhat different time frames and methods. Yet, taken together with findings from other research, including the longitudinal work of Werner and Smith (1992, 2001) in Hawaii, the Fullerton Study of California students (Guerin & Gottfried, 1994), the Bloomington Longitudinal Study (Bates, Maslin, & Frankel, 1985), and the Quebec Temperament Studies (Maziade, Coté, Boutin, Bernier, & Thivierge, 1987), they provide a substantive base for understanding temperament.

Thomas and Chess's 1977 book, *Temperament and Development*, and works by Carey and McDevitt (1994, 1995) contain comprehensive reviews of temperament. Books edited by Halverson, Kohnstamm, and Martin (1994); Kohnstaam, Bates, and Rothbart (1989); Molfese and Molfese (2000); and Wachs and Kohnstaam (2001) also contributed to our understanding of temperament. These books discuss many aspects of temperament including issues of definition, measurement, and clinical implications and applications. I have drawn on these and other research to document how temperament contributes to children's schooling.

HOW THIS BOOK IS ORGANIZED

Much of the research on temperament to date has focused on children and families. Findings from an expanding research base also contain insights about temperament in the context of schooling. In each chapter, I describe research evidence that provides a basis for understanding how knowledge of temperament can improve the school experiences of both students and teachers. I illustrate many ideas with case studies. Additional recommended readings are listed in the bibliography at the end of this book.

Various aspects of temperament are addressed in subsequent chapters. Chapter 2 provides definitions of temperament, including the types and organization of components. Chapter 3 focuses on why temperament is important at home and at school, and Chapter 4 contains a discussion of the basis of individual differences in temperament. Chapters 5 and 6 focus on how temperamental differences contribute to children's and teachers' lives in school, including behavior and adjustment, learning and achievement, and teachers' perceptions and decisions. Temperament and behavior problems are discussed in Chapter 7, and the importance of temperament in children with disabilities is described in Chapter 8. Chapter 9 describes ways temperament can be assessed. Chapter 10, the final chapter, focuses on how temperament can be applied in schools and includes discussion of classroom organization, behavior management, assessment, and interventions.

This book was written for classroom teachers, school psychologists, and other school professionals who work directly with elementary and middle school students. These are important years in children's lives. Think of how many hours are spent in school, of the number of personal and social demands children must face, and of the number of intellectual challenges they must meet. Individual differences in children's attributes influence how well they meet these demands and how well they navigate through the years in school. Intellectual aptitude, motivation, and family support all contribute to children's adjustment and accomplishments. Temperament, or behavior style, is another individual difference that has powerful effects on children's school experiences. My goal is to show how educators' sensitivity to the temperaments of children, as well as to their own, can affect the nature of the classroom interactions, climate, and the quality of school experiences for children and those who teach them.

CHAPTER 2

What Is Temperament?

Classrooms are complex social environments in which children face many demands: what to do, what not to do; when to talk, when to be quiet; when to be active, when to be still. A typical school day is fraught with many distractions and interruptions. Students must respond to many transitions as they go from lessons in reading to lessons in arithmetic, from group activities to individual seat work, and from the playground to the classroom. Often, individual differences in how children manage these demands are clear. Some children are upset by interruptions, whereas others are able to maintain attention and effort. Some adapt quickly and well, whereas others have trouble "settling down." Temperament is one of the personal characteristics that contribute to these differences in classroom behavior. Being aware of these individual differences can alert teachers to potential trouble spots and lead to smoother classroom routines.

As with many other personal characteristics, there are a number of approaches to defining temperament. These approaches reflect, in part at least, the different professional backgrounds and perspectives of those who propose them. They also vary somewhat according to the purposes of the definitions—that is, whether they address clinical or research questions.

DEFINITIONS OF TEMPERAMENT

Despite differences in emphases and specifics, considerable agreement exists among researchers and clinicians about the reality of temperament and the important role it plays in children's experiences.

The New York Longitudinal Study (NYLS) Model of Temperament

One of the most influential definitions of temperament is that of psychiatrists Thomas and Chess (1977) who, as noted in Chapter 1, stressed the stylistic aspects of temperament, or in other words, the *how* of behavior. Their model was based on their clinical experience and on the seminal New York Longitudinal Study, which followed 131 children from age 3 months into adulthood. Thomas and Chess proposed a nine-dimensional model of temperament that identified these temperament characteristics:

Casey is a bright 8-year-old who has many problems in the classroom. He overreacts and is overexcitable. His voice is loud, he talks too much, and he sometimes shouts out answers to the teacher's questions before he has been asked. He intrudes on other children, often interrupting them while they are working on an assignment. He is unpredictable and impatient, sometimes friendly and sometimes complaining and argumentative. On occasion he is physically aggressive, pushing and shoving classmates in order to be first in line or first to play tetherball. He is not well liked and is frequently rejected by classmates.

1. Activity
2. Rhythmicity
3. Approach–withdrawal
4. Adaptability
5. Threshold of responsiveness
6. Intensity
7. Mood
8. Distractibility
9. Persistence

Individuals vary from high to low on each of these dimensions. The nine dimensions and their definitions are found in

Table 2.1. Thomas and Chess argued that temperament is biologically based and that these personal temperament characteristics influenced the interactions between individuals and their environment, particularly the relationships within their families. Their work helped change the prevailing behavioral emphasis in American psychology and education that had focused on environmental influences, paying little attention to biologically based, innate characteristics of the individual.

Thomas and Chess's views on temperament are consistent with the interactional models proposed by psychologists who emphasize that development is neither entirely biologically, maturationally, nor environmentally determined. Clearly, children are influenced *by* their environments, but children also *influence* their environments. One has only to consider how life in a family changes after the birth of a baby or how life in a classroom changes when a few overactive and intense students become part of the group to see how children can affect their environments directly.

> Jason is the most popular child in the class. He is even-tempered, outgoing, and enthusiastic, and he obviously enjoys school. He likes it when something different occurs in the classroom and is excited about the possibility of going on a field trip or doing something special for the teacher. His sense of humor is infectious and he brings a lot of fun to the classroom.

In Thomas and Chess's view, development and behavior are the result of ongoing, continuing interactions and transactions between the individual and the environment. Both contribute to the nature of experience and development, and temperament—or behavioral style—is one of the contributors. Thomas and Chess's nine-dimensional model of temperament has proved to be an especially useful clinical tool in working with families and has stimulated a great deal of research by others.

Other Definitions of Temperament

The model proposed by Thomas and Chess is not the only way to describe temperament; Buss and Plomin defined temperament as

Table 2.1. Temperament categories and definitions according to Thomas and Chess

Category	Definition
Activity level	The motor component present in a given child's functioning and the diurnal proportion of active and inactive periods. Protocol data on motility during bathing, eating, playing, dressing and handling, as well as information concerning the sleep-wake cycle, reaching, crawling and walking, are used in scoring this category.
Rhythmicity (regularity)	The predictability and/or unpredictability in time of any function. It can be analyzed in relation to the sleep-wake cycle, hunger, feeding pattern and elimination schedule.
Approach or withdrawal	The nature of the initial response to a new stimulus, be it a new food, new toy or new person. Approach responses are positive, whether displayed by mood expression (e.g., smiling, verbalizations) or motor activity (e.g., swallowing a new food, reaching for a new toy, active play). Withdrawal reactions are negative, whether displayed by mood expression (e.g., crying, fussing, grimacing, verbalizations) or motor activity (e.g., moving away, spitting new food out, pushing new toy away).
Adaptability	Responses to new or altered situations. One is not concerned with the nature of the initial responses, but with the ease with which they are modified in desired directions.
Threshold of responsiveness	The intensity level of stimulation that is necessary to evoke a discernible response, irrespective of the specific form that the response may take, or the sensory modality affected. The behaviors utilized are those concerning reactions to sensory stimuli, environmental objects, and social contacts.
Intensity of reaction	The energy level of response, irrespective of its quality or direction
Quality of mood	The amount of pleasant, joyful and friendly behavior, as contrasted with unpleasant, crying and unfriendly behavior
Distractibility	The effectiveness of extraneous environmental stimuli in interfering with or in altering the direction of the ongoing behavior
Attention span and persistence	Two categories that are related. Attention span concerns the length of time a particular activity is pursued by the child. Persistence refers to the continuation of an activity in the face of obstacles to the maintenance of the activity direction.

From Thomas, A., & Chess, S. (1977). *Temperament and development* (pp. 21–22). New York: Brunner/Mazel; reprinted by permission.

"broad inherited tendencies" (1975, p. 5) composed of dimensions of emotionality, activity, and sociability. Kagan, Reznick, and Gibbons (1989) considered behavioral inhibition or lack of inhibition to the unfamiliar as temperament qualities, and Goldsmith (1987) argued for emotionality as the defining characteristic. Rothbart (1989) defined temperament in terms of reactivity and self-regulation. Prior, Sanson, Smart, and Oberklaid considered temperament as ". . . individual differences in attentional, emotional, and behavioural self-regulation, along with the relative level of emotional reactivity, which together give a unique flavour to an individual" (2000, p. 3). Rutter referred to "behavioural propensities" (1989, p. 464), and Carey viewed temperament as the "characteristic way that the individual experiences and responds to the internal and external environment" (1989, p. 523). In everyday language, Kurcinka defined temperament as a "preferred style of responding . . . [that is] a child's first and most natural way of responding to the world around him" (1998, p. 25).

Jon is the least-known child in the class. He is unobtrusive and does his school work quietly. He is rarely enthusiastic but is never argumentative or intrusive, and is often overlooked by other children. He is tentative about involving himself in classroom social activities. He is slow to respond to new assignments or to invitations to be part of a group. He has one good friend in the class. They play together on the playground but do not interact a great deal with other children, and indeed, avoid competitive games.

The definitions vary somewhat in specifics and emphases, but share the common recognition that individual differences in temperament are real and that they are relatively enduring. That consensus is captured in the work of Bates, who suggested that in a general sense temperament "consists of biologically rooted individual differences in behavior tendencies that are present early in life and are relatively stable across various kinds of situations and over the course of time" (1989, p. 4).

From a practical perspective, temperament contributes to the uniqueness of individuals. Children may be grouped together according to a particular attribute or talent, yet their temperaments make them unique. For example, a dozen or more students may be in an accelerated eighth-grade arithmetic class because they have exceptionally good skills in math, yet they may bring very different behavioral styles to the group. Some are impulsive and quick to respond, others are deliberate and slow to react; some are high in energy and active physically, others are laid back and sedentary; some are persistent, and others give up quickly. All may be competent, even outstanding achievers in mathematics, yet they are different in temperament. Behavioral style or temperament refers specifically to *how* students behave, not to what they do or how well they do it.

In this book, *temperament* is specifically defined as behavioral style based on the Thomas and Chess model and refers to the characteristic ways individuals respond to and interact with the world around them. The routines of daily living are relatively similar for most people; they involve eating, sleeping, working, studying, and interacting with others. Yet, there are real differences in how individuals carry out these daily activities. Some people are quick, intense, and "fast finishers"; they seem to rush through life. Others are laid-back, tentative, and slow to finish; they seem reflective and deliberate. Differences in children's behavioral styles are apparent while they are eating dinner, completing an assignment in school, or interacting with a parent or teacher. These differences capture the "how" of behavior that makes individuals unique. In this book, the terms *temperament* and *behavioral style* are used interchangeably. Subsequent chapters address the contribution of these stylistic differences to children's achievement and adjustment in school.

THE ORGANIZATION OF TEMPERAMENT DIMENSIONS

In addition to differences in definitions, there are also differences in how the components or the dimensions of temperament are organized—what temperament researchers term "the structure" of temperament. A number of investigators have used statistical techniques to reconfigure the nine Thomas and Chess dimensions, suggesting that some dimensions are related and represent several more basic factors or components. Based on Thomas and Chess's nine dimensions, Keogh, Pullis, and Cadwell (1982) found that teachers' descriptions of children's temperament could be captured in terms of three factors.

1. Factor One, *task orientation*, was made up of dimensions of persistence, distractibility, and activity level. Children high in task orientation were seen as focused, involved in learning tasks, and able to modulate and direct their energies in productive ways—all valued behaviors in a classroom.
2. Factor Two, *personal–social flexibility*, was comprised of temperament dimensions of approach-withdrawal and positive mood. This was essentially a positive factor. These children were characterized as adaptable, as easy to work with, and as friendly and outgoing.
3. Factor Three, composed of dimensions of intensity and threshold of response, was labeled *reactivity*. This was essentially a negative factor. Children rated high on reactivity were described as irritable and as overly responsive and intense—as "prickly."

In the Australian Temperament Project, Sanson, Smart, Prior, Oberklaid, and Pedlow (1994) identified four "strong" and two "less robust" temperament factors. The four strong factors were *inflexibility, persistence, sociability,* and *rhythmicity.* The less robust factors were *activity/mood* and *threshold.* The strong factors were "pure" statistically and conceptually. They made sense when interpreted, and they were consistent across the age range of 3–7 years. In contrast, the weaker factors were "mixed," were less clear conceptually, and varied by age. For example, activity was related to reactivity in infants but to intensity in toddlers, according to Sanson et al., and distractibility was a factor only in toddlers. The Australian researchers found some differences in structure related to social class, culture, and ethnicity (see Chapter 3). The structure was similar for boys and girls across the ages studied, but some differences in the expression of temperament according to gender were apparent. Boys were found to be somewhat less flexible and less persistent than were girls, whereas girls were "... more active/cheerful/sensitive" (1994, p. 244). These researchers suggested that inflexibility is a core aspect of "difficultness." Certainly, teachers often find that inflexible students present problems in the classroom because they do not cope well with the many ongoing changes in classroom demands.

Dunedin researchers Caspi, Henry, McGee, Moffitt, and Silva (1995) analyzed behavioral styles based on observations of one group of children as they developed from ages 3 to 9, finding that children's behavioral styles could be described by three factors: *lack of control, approach,* and *sluggishness.* The lack of control factor tapped aspects of emotional lability, short attention span, and negativism, and was related to difficulty in modulating impulsive behaviors and in persisting on tasks. These characteristics are seen in children in the classroom who call out answers inappropriately, who have difficulty sitting still and staying in their seats, and who wander about the room, often disturbing others.

The approach factor captured children's styles of responding to others and to new situations. Approachable children are at ease in social situations in the classroom and on the playground; adjust quickly to new assignments and new routines; and are outgoing, self-confident, and willing and eager to explore. In contrast, the sluggishness factor characterized children who were shy and fearful, who tended to be passive, who were "flat" emotionally, and who were less involved socially.

The three factors described by Caspi and colleagues were relatively independent and generally consistent with behavioral styles identified by other researchers of temperament. Some differences in the specific number and make up of components and in terminology can be found in the work of different researchers, however. For example, Buss and Plomin (1975) identified three primary components of temperament, whereas Thomas and Chess identified nine dimensions. Rothbart (1989) focused on reactivity and self-regulation, whereas Goldsmith (1987) considered temperament as emotionality.

Despite differences, there is considerable agreement. Based on examination of different conceptualizations, McClowry (1995) identified four primary components of temperament that are consistently found in most definitions. The first refers to a *social* component, which describes children's social responses to others. Other names for this component include approach/withdrawal, personal–social flexibility, and sociability. A second common factor relates to persistence—a child's ability to maintain effort and attention. This temperament dimension is also referred to as task orientation, attention span–persistence, or task persistence. A third factor found in most definitions has to do with negative affect, sometimes called negative emotionality, inflexibility, or reactivity. A final component relates to activity, including—but not limited—to motor activity. McClowry suggested that this component might more accurately be called *energy*, as it describes, ". . . how school-age children expend and exhibit their propensity toward activity" (1995, p. 274).

Factors identified in several conceptualizations are summarized in Table 2.2. McClowry's fourth component, activity or energy, is found in most conceptualizations but is represented in different factors.

The temperament dimensions and factors described previously allow teachers to develop a picture or profile of individual children. For example, one child might be seen as high in activity and low in persistence and approach. Another child in the same classroom might be low in activity but high in persistence and approach. These two children will likely differ in how they respond to instruction: the former needing help in focusing and staying on task, the latter being more independent and able to complete assignments on his or her own. Considering child-

Table 2.2. Temperament factors as identified by researchers

Researchers	Factors
Keogh, Pullis, & Cadwell (1982)	Task orientation
	Adaptability
	Reactivity
Sanson, Smart, Prior, Oberklaid, & Pedlow (1994)	Persistence
	Inflexibility
	Sociability
	Rythmicity (activity, mood)
Caspi, Henry, McGee, Moffitt, & Silva (1995)	Lack of control
	Approach
	Sluggishness
McClowry (1995)	Social response
	Persistence
	Negative affect
	Activity

ren's characteristics on the temperament dimensions or factors alerts teachers to differences in children's needs. Profiles provide a useful way of summarizing temperament information, and they increase sensitivity to individual characteristics within each child as well as alerting teachers to individual differences among children.

Temperament Types

Another way to think about temperament is to describe types or groups of children who exhibit similar temperament patterns. The goal in this approach is to identify clusters of individuals who are temperamentally as much alike as possible, but who also differ as much as possible from other groups or clusters of individuals. Researchers have used both clinical and statistical techniques to identify relatively homogeneous clusters of children based on their temperaments. This approach results in the description of types of individuals who are temperamentally similar to each other but who differ from other temperament types. Three typologies are illustrative.

Based on their clinical expertise, Thomas and Chess (1977) described three primary constellations of temperament characteristics that they viewed as having "functional significance" in children's experiences within their families. These types were based on the nine dimensions listed in their model. Almost two-thirds of the children could be described as belonging to one of the three groups.

Easy "Easy" children are characterized by regularity, adaptability to change, positive response to newness, mild to moderate intensity, and positive mood. They are friendly, social, and outgoing children who are responsive to others and who are not easily frustrated or angry. It is not surprising that they are well liked by teachers and peers. Approximately 40% of the children in the New York Longitudinal Study were considered "easy."

Difficult "Difficult" children are characterized by biological irregularity, negative mood, low adaptability to change, intensity of reactions, and negative response to newness. These children tend to overreact, to be unpredictable, and to be quickly frustrated when things don't go their way. Teachers often find them irritable and irritating, as they may not adapt readily to classroom rules and routines and may have problems getting along with classmates. Approximately 10% of the children in the Thomas and Chess study were in that cluster.

Slow-to-Warm-Up "Slow-to-warm-up" children have the predominant characteristics of mild negative response to newness coupled with slow adaptability to change. These slow starters often need special support and patience because they tend to stand back rather than get involved. In the Thomas and Chess study, 15% of the children participating fell into this category.

Parent–child and teacher–child interactions are affected by these temperament constellations. Life at home and at school is much smoother with easy children than with difficult ones. A highly active, intense, and impulsive child like Casey is not always fun to be with, for example, on a family driving trip. Similarly, teachers will have their hands full when Casey is part of the group on an all-day field trip to the museum. His activity level and impulsiveness can lead him to rush off from the group or to intrude and interrupt the museum docent who guides the tour. In contrast, Jon may need encouragement and special attention because he is bothered by new situations and tends to lag behind his classmates. The notion of describing individuals in terms of being easy, difficult, and slow to warm up has been applied in medical, educational, and psychological contexts, and findings converge to suggest that individual differences in temperament evoke different responses from adults and peers (see Carey & McDevitt, 1995, for discussion).

Another effort to identify temperament types comes from the Dunedin study of New Zealand children. Recall that researchers in that study identified three major temperament factors: lack of control, approach, and sluggishness. The children were grouped according to their temperament profiles using statistical cluster-analytic methods (Caspi & Silva, 1995). The series of analyses yielded five clusters that identified children with similar temperaments or stylistic patterns: 1) undercontrolled, 2) inhibited, 3) confident, 4) sluggish, and 5) well-adjusted.

Undercontrolled   The first cluster, called *undercontrolled*, contained more boys than girls. The children in this cluster received high scores on items describing difficulty sitting still, variability of responses, low control of their behavior, rough behavior, and problems sustaining attention. These children stood out in a crowded classroom.

Inhibited   The second cluster, termed *inhibited*, was made up of children who were high on lack of control but who also had high scores on sluggishness. These children were characterized as inhibited in new situations, as shy and fearful, and as having limited communication with others; they were also described as distractible, with problems in sustaining attention. More girls than boys made up this cluster.

Confident   Cluster three, labeled *confident*, was composed of children who were especially strong in approach and eager to explore and try new things. These children were responsive and interactive with others and adjusted quickly to newness. Boys and girls were almost evenly represented in this cluster.

Sluggish   In contrast to the Confident cluster, children making up cluster four, *sluggish*, were described as moderately shy, fearful, and self-critical. Although timid, these children's behaviors were not extreme and they were adequately task oriented and able to sustain attention. Slightly more girls than boys were included in this cluster.

Well-Adjusted   The children making up cluster five, *well-adjusted*, were considered to be typical of their age peers. Although in many ways similar to the confident children, they were not as extreme. They were seen as average or normative in self-confidence and task orientation, willing to attempt assignments, friendly, self-controlled, and not overly upset by difficulty. This fifth cluster contained the largest number of children and slightly more boys than girls.

Still another statistical approach to identification of temperament types is found in the research of Martin and Bridger (1999). They based their typologies on assessment data from the Temperament Assessment Battery for Children–Revised (TABC-R, 1999). They found that parent and teacher responses on the TABC-R yielded six clusters or types: *inhibited* (constrained in responsiveness to others), *highly emotional* (anxious and impulsive, high levels of negative emotionality), *impulsive* (problems with self-regulation and control), *typical* (moderate levels of impulsivity and inhibition), *reticent* (quiet, unobtrusive and sociable), and *uninhibited* (self-regulating, positive emotionality and sociability).

Temperament types from these three studies are summarized in Table 2.3. Though differences are found in the number and

Table 2.3. Temperament types as identified by researchers

Researchers	Factors
Thomas and Chess (1977)	Easy
	Difficult
	Slow to warm up
Caspi and Silva (1995)	Undercontrolled
	Inhibited
	Confident
	Sluggish
	Well-adjusted
Martin and Bridger (1999)	Inhibited
	Highly emotional
	Impulsive
	Typical
	Reticent
	Uninhibited

specificity of types, there is also considerable agreement and over-lap across studies, a finding that supports the usefulness of types as a way of thinking about individual differences in temperament.

HOW DOES TEMPERAMENT AFFECT LIFE IN THE CLASSROOM?

In light of these researchers' findings, the impact of different temperaments on classroom management and instruction is important to consider. Wouldn't most teachers like to have a classroom of students who are confident and well adjusted in the way that Caspi and Silva described these terms? "Easy" children make for smooth-running and positive classrooms where teaching can be emphasized. In contrast, the presence of a number of impulsive, uninhibited, and undercontrolled students can lead to challenges in establishing and maintaining classroom routines and order, resulting in classrooms where behavior management rather than instruction is a priority. From a different perspective, inhibited, reticent, and "sluggish" students can pose particular concerns for teachers, especially when new instructional materials and methods are introduced. Those children may need special encouragement and support.

Of course, teachers cannot choose their students, and all children deserve the best education possible. Classroom life is composed of many ingredients, including children's intellectual, motivational, and physical characteristics. Individual differences in students' temperaments are also important in the classroom mix, and teachers necessarily must respond to all of these individual differences on a day-by-day basis. It is no wonder that teaching is such a demanding task. Becoming aware of individual differences in children's temperaments can broaden teachers' views of children's competencies and problems and can lead to insights that will improve the school experiences for both students and teachers.

SUMMARY

Findings from a number of research groups provide consistent evidence documenting the reality of temperament as an individual characteristic. The definitions vary somewhat in detail and in emphasis, but there is considerable overlap in the dimensions and components described. There is also agreement that individual differences in temperament have some biological basis, that these differences are apparent early in life, and that temperament contributes to the ways individuals experience their worlds. The interactional nature of temperament and environment has been well described in the context of family life, but it deserves serious consideration in the context of school, a point of view elaborated in subsequent chapters in this book.

CHAPTER 3

Why Understanding Temperament Is Important

Chapter 1 describes temperament as the "how" of behavior. Important questions surround the ways in which stylistic temperament differences affect children's experiences. In this regard, Teglasi (1998) suggested that children's temperaments contribute to their development and behavior in several ways. Temperament influences how individuals select activities and environments; it shapes the responses of others, and it modifies the impact of the environment. Recall how differently Raoul and Stevie, the two 5-year-olds described in Chapter 1, approached the first day of kindergarten. Raoul immediately and enthusiastically came into the classroom and was quickly involved with other children. Stevie stood back and waited and watched, and after some time, carefully and tentatively joined the group.

The role of temperament in children's experiences is best understood from an *interactionist* perspective. In the late 1960s, Bell (1968) argued persuasively that adult–child relationships are bidirectional and interactive. That is, children are affected by the behavior of adults, but children also affect adults' behavior.

Historically, clinicians and researchers have focused on the influence of adults, especially parents, on children. The effects of family environments and parenting styles have been well researched, and as part of this work, a range of family influences have been identified as contributing to healthy development as well as to children's psychiatric and conduct problems (see Lewis & Feiring, 1998). Positive family influences include firm but supportive parenting styles, warm and accepting family climates, and stable home environments. In their 40-year longitudinal study, Werner and Smith (2001) found that the adults who had been in high-risk environments as children and who coped well as adults tended to come from smaller families, had older and better educated mothers, and had strong relationships with caring adults in extended families or in the community, including teachers.

Negative family influences have also been identified such as high levels of stress and adversity and poor parenting styles. Sameroff, Bartko, Baldwin, Baldwin, and Seifer (1998), for example, identified family and social conditions that influenced the development of competence in children in the Rochester Longitudinal Study. Environmental risk variables such as maternal mental illness, rigid parental ideas about children's development, low levels of parental education and occupation, and large family size were all associated with troubling developmental outcomes. Clearly, familial and parental attributes have a major impact on children's development and well-being.

That is not the complete story, however. Adults alone do not determine a child's environment. Children also contribute. Development is an ongoing process in which child and environment interact with and affect each other.

Leticia's parents and teachers describe her as highly active, intense, and over-reactive. She is quick to cry when she feels she is being criticized and is often moody. She also has a short attention span. Some days her parents feel that they spend most of their home hours catering to Leticia. Though they love her very much, they are often exhausted from trying to keep her happy and occupied.

As youngsters, the successful adults from high-risk backgrounds in the Werner and Smith study (2001) were described as approaching, sociable, responsive, and agreeable, personal attributes that helped them cope with negative environmental conditions. From this perspective children are not just passive victims of their social conditions, but rather they influence—even shape—their environments and the behaviors of others. Thus, one must consider both the characteristics of children and the characteristics of the context in which they live and go to school in order to understand how individual differences in temperament contribute to children's behavior and adjustment.

HOW TEMPERAMENT CONTRIBUTES TO EXPERIENCE

From an interactionist perspective, children's personal attributes, including temperament, serve both active and evocative roles. Scarr described active roles as "niche-picking." That is, people ". . . seek out environments they find compatible and stimulating; they live in them, enlarge and deepen them" (1981, p. 1163). Some children actively seek physical activity and competition and feel comfortable in athletics and physically demanding situations. Some may even seek "risky" activities, finding these exciting and stimulating. Other children avoid competitive or risky experiences and seek quieter, less interactive situations. Consider the scholarly child who is most comfortable when pursuing his interests alone in the library or the socially oriented child who is happiest when with people and bored and unhappy when alone. These differences appear more related to temperament than to cognitive or physical attributes, and they clearly affect the nature of children's lives.

Rutter (1989) also noted that individual differences in temperament affect the range of children's experiences. A high-approach, friendly child will seek out social situations, whereas a timid, withdrawing child will avoid them. An active, impulsive child may involve him- or herself in activities that could lead to negative consequences, whereas a more reflective and inhibited child will not engage in them. This suggests that individual differences in children's temperaments influence what they do and how they do it and that these differences among children contribute to their range of experiences over time.

Another way temperament affects children's experiences refers to how individual differences in children's behavioral styles evoke reactions from others. Children's characteristics, including temperament, elicit different responses from both adults and peers and, thus, influence the nature of children's personal and social interactions. Some children evoke negative, punitive responses from adults; others evoke positive and supportive responses. Most parents agree that "easy" children are more compatible with everyday family life than are "difficult" children, and "slow-to-warm-up" children as described by Thomas and Chess (1977) may present different challenges to family activities and routines. The result is that children are treated differently, even in the same family.

The same generalizations can be made about classrooms and teachers' interactions with children. Within a classroom environment, some children get more attention from the teacher than do others. More importantly, perhaps, teachers' affective, instructional, and behavioral responses to their students differ dramatically. Some children enjoy positive and friendly relationships with teachers while others receive teachers' attention primarily for management and instructional purposes. These interactions vary, in part, because children's temperaments evoke different responses from teachers.

Simply put, teachers "like" and get along with some children better than others, and temperament is part of that equation. Most teachers find task-oriented and approaching children easier to teach than children who withdraw in the face of new assignments or who are inflexible and negative. Most teachers prefer to have in their classroom children who are adaptable and moderate in intensity rather than those who are distractible and highly reactive.

GOODNESS OF FIT

Viewing temperament and classroom life from an interactionist perspective captures the notion of *goodness of fit*, a concept that is central in understanding why temperament is important. Thomas and Chess defined goodness of fit in terms of the nature of the interactions of individual and environment. They suggested that interactions might result in positive or negative outcomes depending on whether ". . . the properties of the environment and its expectations and demands are in accord with the organism's own capacities, characteristics, and style of behaving" (1977, p. 11). Healthy developmental and positive personal outcomes are likely to follow when there is a good fit between the child's characteristics and the environment, whereas the probability of negative consequences increases when there is a poor fit. The notion of goodness of fit holds that one must think about context as well as the characteristics of the child.

Classroom Environments, Instructional Programs, and Goodness of Fit

The bulk of research on temperament and goodness of fit has been directed at families, but it is obvious that goodness of fit also plays a powerful role in schools. We must consider classroom contexts and teachers' temperaments as well as student characteristics. Keogh and Speece (1996) proposed that three aspects of classrooms are important in the fit between students and classroom environments: 1) the content and nature of the curriculum and modes of instruction; 2) the organization and management of space, time, and resources; and 3) the nature of the interactions between students, peers, and teachers. These three components of the classroom interact with students' temperaments as well as with students' interests and abilities. In some cases these interactions lead to a productive match; in other cases they lead to problems. In addition, it is likely that a child's cultural and ethnic background interacts with his or her temperament in the goodness-of-fit equation, a point to be discussed later in this chapter.

Content and Nature of Curriculum   Classrooms are organized differently according to teachers' views of how instruction should be delivered and their ideas about whether children should learn through exploration or direct teaching. Consider how the match between students' cognitive abilities and subject-matter skills and the level and content of the instructional program affect learning. Students may be frustrated or bored when the content and level of the curriculum are discrepant from their abilities. Other children face near-impossible obstacles to learning because their reading or arithmetic skills are discrepant from the demands of the curriculum, or because the teacher's instructional style and strategies do not match the students' aptitudes and needs.

Organization of Space, Time, and Resources   Goodness of fit is not limited to academics and instruction. It also refers to larger aspects of the classroom environment and to how that environment interacts with children's temperaments to affect behavior. In every classroom many ongoing activities are taking place. Students are often in crowded rooms buzzing with small talk. Some children may be involved in a small group discussing a special project while others do individual work at their desks or work center. Some children may be getting individual help from the teacher or aide while still others are idle, doodling, or even daydreaming. During any given time period, there are many interruptions and potential distractions: A student is slow in coming back from doing an errand for the teacher. The principal makes an announcement over the loudspeaker. A student monitor collects money for a class party. Three boys are clowning around in the back of the room, and the teacher is describing plans for an upcoming field trip.

How individual children respond to these conditions is, in part, related to temperament. Some children may withdraw or misbehave when the classroom is overly structured—some, when it is chaotic. It is not surprising that reactive and impersistent children will find overly rigid or chaotic classroom environments difficult for learning; that shy and withdrawing children will become increasingly anxious, quiet, and noncommunicative in environments that are high activity and high stimulation; or that intense and excitable children will have difficulty regulating their own behavior in the same classroom. Examples of fit or lack of fit between children and the organization and routines of the classroom are everywhere.

Nature of Interactions
Between Students, Peers, and Teachers

Classrooms are very public places. Children are well aware of others' successes and failures as well as of their own and are sensitive to how teachers respond to different students. Ask any classroom of third or fourth graders to tell you who is the best reader, who is the best artist, who is the most "trouble," and you will find almost unanimous agreement. As Erickson (1996) points out, the very public nature of performance in school makes it "risky business" for many children. The risk may be greatest for the child who is temperamentally shy and withdrawing because such children are often uncomfortable and ill at ease when in the spotlight. Conversely, the temperamentally outgoing and exuberant child may find the attention positive and reinforcing.

It is important to remember that teachers' individual differences in temperaments affect their interactions with students. Just like children, some educators are outgoing, exuberant, and active; others are quiet; some are even dour. These teacher characteristics contribute to the affective environments of classrooms as well as to the fit with individual children. (This point is elaborated in Chapter 10.)

Cultural and Ethnic Background Still another aspect of context has to do with ethnic/cultural influences and temperament. Prior, Garino, Sanson, and Oberklaid (1987) found differences in ratings of infants' temperaments among mothers and caregivers from thirteen different ethnic groups living in Australia. Immigrants included families from the United Kingdom, Europe, Asia, the Middle East, Africa, and North America. In general, the infant temperament ratings of parents who had emigrated from Britain and North America were similar to those of native Australian parents. Differences were found for a number of other ethnic groups, however, especially regarding how the mothers in those groups rated their children on dimensions of approach, adaptability, and distractibility. These findings suggested that there may be differences in how difficultness is viewed relative to ethnic/cultural backgrounds.

Hertzig, Birch, Thomas, and Mendez (1968) observed differences between parents in the New York Longitudinal Study (NYLS) and parents of Puerto Rican backgrounds living in New York City in the behaviors they valued in their young children. The Puerto Rican families were more "person" oriented, emphasizing social behavior. The NYLS parents were more "independence" oriented, emphasizing self-help skills. Super and Harkness (1994) documented differences in the constellation of temperament characteristics that were viewed as difficult by rural African families and by urban American families. Difficult infants in the NYLS were described as intense, negative, and arrhythmic, whereas the difficult infants in rural Africa were those who

Kyong comes from a home in which children are expected to be quiet and respectful. Her teacher, Mr. Blair, seems to value outgoing, funny students. Kyong feels that she doesn't fit in well in such a class, and has trouble getting into the class activities because of difficulties in adjusting to Mr. Blair's boisterous, casual manner.

were easily upset and slow to be comforted. In both instances, however, the infants' behavior had negative effects on the daily routines of family life. Clearly, "difficultness" is best understood against a backdrop of cultural differences.

It is interesting to note, however, that despite findings of specific differences among cultural groups, consistencies exist in the ways temperament is interpreted across cultures, leading de-Vries to propose that difficult temperament is a "universal and culturally embedded concept" (1989, p. 81). He pointed out that difficultness is recognized in many cultures, and that it has its basis in "troublesome" temperamental characteristics that interfere with the daily lives and activities of caregivers. The specific temperamental attributes and the responses to them vary according to cultural group and to the nature of the everyday business of adults, but a common constellation of characteristics making up "difficultness" includes poor adaptability, high reactivity, intensity of response, and negative mood. Children with those characteristics are apt to be perceived as troublesome in many contexts, including school, because they upset daily routines and require special attention.

The idea of culturally related differences in how temperament is viewed is especially relevant to school. Classrooms are filled with students from many different cultural and ethnic backgrounds. They come to school from homes with particular expectations about what is acceptable or unacceptable behavior, and about the meaning and importance of particular temperamental characteristics. Teachers, too, come with unique temperaments that reflect their own cultural beliefs and values. In some cases, the two will mesh well; in other cases, the two will be discrepant, leading to misunderstandings and stress.

In some cultures, children who are energetic, active, intense, and persistent are highly valued and admired; other cultures find these same characteristics troublesome, especially when they clash with gender-based expectations (G. Axia, personal communication, 2001). Indeed, it is likely that certain behaviors and temperamental characteristics are acceptable or not acceptable according to culturally based beliefs about what boys "should" be like and what girls "should" be like. These differences may be especially important influences in how children's behaviors are interpreted in school. Parents may see particular patterns of temperament as evidence of assertiveness and individuality. Teachers may see the same temperament as the basis for aggressive and disruptive behavior.

These interpretations of temperament underscore the point that individual differences in children's temperament may be viewed differently depending on where children are and what is expected of them. Cultural differences in how a child's behavior is viewed may lead to misunderstandings and disagreements in parent–teacher conferences about a child who is having problems in school, and may disrupt plans for needed services. These differences may be increasingly important as the school population becomes more culturally diverse.

Taken as a whole, the findings about culture and temperament illustrate Super and Harkness's point that ". . . different kinds of environments find various temperaments differentially suitable, and . . . within any type of environment various temperaments elicit different responses" (1994, p. 117). These generalizations are relevant when considering differences in the cultures of home and school. They are also relevant when considering temperament *within* schools. Schools and classrooms within schools may be remarkably different, and students and teachers bring different attributes to these contexts. A child's temperament may be seen as positive by one teacher but may be troublesome to another. Teachers may differ in how they interpret a child's temperament, one valuing the child's behavioral style, another finding it disruptive or negative. This of course, underscores the importance of goodness of fit.

Temperament Differences and Goodness of Fit

Carey and McDevitt (1995) make an interesting point about the way individual differences in temperament affect the goodness of fit between child and environment. They noted that "easy" children are apt to get along in many situations, whereas "difficult" children fit a narrower range of environments. Some children are at ease, relaxed, and happy in almost every situation and with many different people. Fox, Henderson, Rubin, Calkins, and Schmidt (2001) described "exuberant" children as approaching, social, interested in novelty, and lacking in fear, characteristics that make for positive and successful relationships at home and in school. In contrast, inhibited children may be content and at ease only when at home or with a few select people. These individual differences in temperament can affect the breadth of children's experiences as well as their fit with the environment.

Dalton is an intense, active, and impulsive 9-year-old boy. In his classroom, in which routines are very rigid and assignments are long, he has trouble sitting in his seat and staying on task. Having to stand in line for long periods of time is an invitation to trouble for this child and often leads to negative interchanges with his teacher.

In this regard, it is important to emphasize that the pattern and intensity of a child's temperament and the flexibility of the environment are both key components in the "goodness" or "badness" of fit. Not all children with difficult temperaments are similar in intensity or negative mood. As Carey and McDevitt suggested, "The stronger, the more pervasive, and the less modifiable the characteristic, the greater the chances that the child's temperament will be incompatible with any setting" (1995, p. 14). A seriously withdrawing, inflexible child may have problems in almost any classroom because transitions and change are part of everyday classroom life. The impact of these personal styles may be intensified by particular classroom environments and by the interactions with the teacher who designs and maintains that environment.

The impact of temperament may also be seen in other situations in school. Consider children with low thresholds of responsiveness who are especially sensitive to sights and sounds in the environment. Eating lunch in the school cafeteria can be traumatic for these children because the noises, smells, clatter, and confusion can be overstimulating and overwhelming. A field trip to a local museum may be exciting and interesting for most children but upsetting to others because it means a change in the usual routines and activities. Still other children may be overstimulated and overwhelmed by the many displays and activities found in most museums.

Temperament is certainly not the only attribute that affects goodness of fit—children's gender, age, and intelligence also contribute. Indeed, many factors likely work in combination. For example, shyness or behavioral inhibition may be more acceptable in girls than in boys. Intense, highly active, and impulsive girls may be seen as more difficult for parents and teachers than boys displaying the same behaviors. Gender has also been shown to affect students' learning opportunities, as girls may be counseled away from careers in math and science. Research by the American Association of University Women (AAUW, 1992) found that compared with boys, girls received less attention, support, and encouragement from teachers and were given fewer opportunities to use their abilities. The report suggested that girls were "shortchanged" in many classrooms. As noted earlier, temperament attributes may have different meanings in specific cultural groups. The temperaments of individual children may not fit well with culturally defined gender role expectations for school behavior and performance, leading to misunderstandings and problems, a point discussed in more detail in later chapters.

In sum, the idea of goodness of fit has been applied to children's development, to clinical problems, and to family interactions. (See Carey & McDevitt, 1994, 1995; and Chess & Thomas, 1999, for discussions.) It is equally important in schooling. The idea that the meaning and relevance of temperament is situationally embedded is captured by this quotation from Thomas, Chess, and Birch:

> In themselves, temperamental attributes are neither good nor bad. Whether a given temperament trait of a child meets with approval

or disapproval, results in praise or criticism, or proves convenient or inconvenient to adults and peers can depend upon its appropriateness to the situations in which it is expressed and upon the degree to which its manifestations correspond to the value judgments of others. (1968, p. 100)

TEMPERAMENT CHARACTERISTICS AS RISK AND PROTECTIVE INFLUENCES

Still another aspect of temperament has to do with its effect as a risk or protective influence. A large body of research documents environmental and contextual conditions that increase the risk for children's development (see Lewis & Feiring, 1998). These include physical, social, and psychological factors in families and in schools, and they are clearly powerful contributors to children's well being. Consistent with an interactionist perspective, the effects of adverse conditions also vary relative to the characteristics of the individual, and temperament is one of the important "in-child" characteristics. That is, individual differences in children's temperaments may predispose them to positive or negative interactions with their environments. Indeed, temperament may have a particularly powerful influence when children are in adverse situations. An intense, impulsive, and highly active child is more apt to "act out" when home or school conditions are chaotic or stressful than when conditions are calm and orderly. A shy and inhibited child may become more withdrawn when classroom conditions are unorganized and inconsistent.

Risk Factors

Temperament may put a child at risk at home or at school. Pediatrician Carey (1989) suggested that temperament could predispose a child to disorders of nutrition and growth as well as to functional disorders such as sleep problems. Keogh (1983) described relationships between students' task orientation and their achievement in school. This is not surprising given that that factor of task orientation is composed of persistence, distractibility, and activity level.

Temperament may also contribute to later adjustment problems, especially when the temperament attributes are extreme. Canadian psychiatrist Maziade (1994) and his research group have documented links between extreme temperament characteristics of low adaptability, high withdrawal, intensity, distractibility, and negative mood in the early years and externalizing behavior problems as the children grow older. These findings are, of course, consistent with the earlier reports by Thomas and Chess (1977) and Thomas, Chess, and Birch (1968), who found that temperament in the early years was often related to later adjustment problems in the school and adolescent years.

Like other researchers, Maziade (1994) cautioned that not all young children with extremely difficult temperaments develop problems, nor do all children with problems exhibit this pattern of temperament. He stressed that problems are a consequence of both child characteristics and environmental conditions and emphasized the importance of taking both into account when working clinically with children and their families. As a researcher-clinician, Maziade argued that the fact of individual differences in temperament cannot be ignored when there are problems, but that recognition of temperamental differences changes the often-held view that parents are to blame for the behavior problems of their children. A positive clinical benefit of acknowledging individual differences in temperament is that it can reduce the guilt parents often feel when their children have problems. It also points the way to individualizing the ways they work with their child. Maziade noted, "No good and general principle of management can apply indiscriminately to every child" (p. 17), a generalization appropriately applied at home and at school to parents and to teachers and counselors.

Taken as whole, the findings argue for considering particular temperaments as potential risk influences that increase the likelihood of problems at home and at school, especially when environmental conditions are stressful.

Protective Factors

Remember that temperament characteristics can also be protective influences. Garmezy, Masten, and Tellegen defined *protective factors* as ". . . dispositional attributes, environmental conditions, biological predispositions, and positive events that can contain the expression of deviance . . ." (1984, p. 109). Protective factors buffer negative conditions and enhance positive coping. Both contextual and in-child characteristics serve as positive influences on development and adjustment, and temperament is one of these characteristics. Researchers in the Australian Temperament Project, for example, found that positive temperament was an important protective influence for children in stressful conditions. Children who were seen as competent and coping well despite adverse family environments were temperamentally different from those children who fared less well. The competent children were more task oriented, had good emotional control, and were more persistent. They had better relationships with their families and peers, and were seen by their mothers as "easier to live with." Prior, Sanson, Smart, and Oberklaid, concluded that ". . . those characteristics that we call temperamental self-regulation (persistence and flexibility) and positive emotionality clearly play a very significant role as 'protective' or supportive factors for individuals experiencing adversity, in helping them to remain well adjusted" (2000, p. 37).

Whether temperament serves as a risk or a protective influence is, at least in part, related to the interactions of child characteristics and conditions in the environment. This is true both at home and at school. Certainly an intense, active, and reactive child may be at risk for adjustment difficulties in a particular school classroom. Yet, the same temperament attributes may serve as protective influences in other situations, even in a different classroom and with a different teacher. The behavior and adjustment of some children may change from year to year according to their classrooms, as well. The "problem child" in kindergarten may do well in first grade, whereas the successful elementary school child may have problems meeting the more complex demands of middle school.

Difficult temperament deserves particular comment in this regard, as it is usually viewed as a cluster of negative characteristics that increase the likelihood of problems. Yet, the attributes making up difficultness may be protective in some circumstances. The point is dramatically illustrated in anthropologist deVries's description of a study of temperament in several African groups. He documented that many of the characteristics (e.g. highly active, fussy, nonadaptive, assertive) that made a child difficult and "at risk" in Western cultures were actually protective. deVries found that African Masai infants who survived a terrible drought in which many of the tribal infants perished could be described as difficult. The demanding, difficult children were fed, whereas the more docile and less difficult infants were not, which illustrates a kind of "squeaky wheel" effect. In fact, deVries noted that "Under the extreme circumstances . . . instead of being a risk factor, difficult temperament proved to be protective in this period of drought and . . . high mortality . . ." (1994, p. 130).

Although not as dramatic as deVries's report, Carey (1985) found accelerated weight gain in infants with difficult temperaments, suggesting that caregivers were likely feed them often as a way of soothing them. From a different perspective, Keogh, Bernheimer, and Guthrie (1997) found differences in the cognitive growth patterns of children with developmental delays that favored the difficult rather than the easy children. A reasonable inference is that temperamentally easy children in that study were less demanding than difficult children, and that the difficult children had more interactions with caregivers and thus received more stimulation.

This inference is well illustrated by Carey and McDevitt (1995), who analyzed how extremes of each of the nine temperament dimensions proposed by Thomas and Chess may be positive or negative, that is, how each can be a risk or a protective influence in children's behavior and adjustment. They suggested, for example, that on the one hand, high activity might put a child at risk if the activity is purposeless and disorganized and interferes with task performance and social activities. Low activity can also be a risk influence because it may be interpreted as laziness or lethargy. On the other hand, they noted that high activity may be protective if it leads to vigorous interactions and to stimulating exploratory behaviors, whereas low activity might be protective by making a child "less obtrusive" in restrictive environments. Similarly, a child who has high approach tendencies (i.e., who engages with people and new situations easily and willingly) might be risky because they sometimes put him or her in a "hazardous environment," whereas a tendency toward low approach may lead a child to avoid many positive experiences. What makes particular environments hazardous is in part related to children's temperaments and will be different for different children. Some children's temperaments may predispose them to be accident prone, whereas others are rarely hurt. For example, Plumet and Schwebel (1997) found that parents reported more accidents for children who overestimated their physical abilities and who were low in self-regulation and inhibitory control than for children with different personal characteristics.

Risky environments are not limited to possible physical accidents, of course, as other environments may be potentially hazardous for children with particular temperaments. Children who are very high approach may place themselves in danger by being too comfortable with potentially dangerous strangers, for example.

The risk and protective roles of temperament must be viewed from an interactionist perspective.

Benjy, a small, wiry 10-year-old who is impulsive and high in energy, has problems modulating his behavior. He loves physical activity, especially challenging activities. He is a fearless skateboarder and an avid bike rider and skier. He consistently attempts difficult and demanding feats, sometimes getting into potentially dangerous situations. He has had several nasty accidents when jumping high curbs on his skateboard, and his parents had to ground him for riding his bike at full speed on a road with heavy automobile traffic.

This may be especially true when children's behavior and adjustment in school are considered. Classrooms differ in organization, routines, and demands, and students are expected to respond appropriately to those differences. Because students differ in abilities and temperaments, educators should expect that in any classroom there will be real differences in how well the child's characteristics fit with the teacher's expectations, and with the demands of the program. Thus, understanding how temperament contributes to behavior and adjustment requires consideration of classroom, child, and teacher characteristics, including temperament.

TEMPERAMENT AND RESILIENCE

A particularly interesting aspect of protective influences relates to the idea of resilience. Stories abound of children who develop and achieve well in conditions that result in negative outcomes for most individuals. These children are described as *resilient*, a term that refers to individuals who have the "... capacity to maintain healthy functioning in an unhealthy setting" or the "... capacity ... to recover, bounce back, or remain buoyant in the face of adversity, life stresses, illness, misfortune, and the like" (Smith & Prior, 1995, p. 168).

In their remarkable 40-year study of a cohort of individuals growing up on the Hawaiian island of Kauai, Werner and Smith (2001) found that approximately one third of the individuals in their study were considered to be "at risk" as children because of biological and environmental conditions. A number of children included in the study did have problems as older children and adolescents. These problems included poor achievement in school, delinquent behavior, and mental health problems. Not all of the high-risk individuals developed behavior or learning problems, however, and about 1 out of every 10 children in the Kauai study was considered "resilient." These resilient individuals were described in infancy as having positive temperaments, as being good natured and easy to care for, and as affectionate and active. As toddlers they had positive social orientations and enjoyed novelty, and as elementary school children, they were well liked and had many interests and activities. Throughout the years, these individuals coped well with the stresses in their environments, and as adults they were "competent, confident, and caring persons" (2001, p. 56). Certainly, temperament was not the only characteristic that described them, but temperament was a particularly important influence on their development and adjustment in the early years, perhaps serving as a protective influence for individuals in adverse circumstances.

Smith and Prior (1995) also found that temperament attributes differed for the resilient and nonresilient Australian children whom they studied, although all were from stressed environments. In general, resilient children were seen as "engaging," as having easy and positive temperaments, and as being attractive to others, including children and adults. The resilient children were socially responsive, drew people to them, had low levels of excitability and distress, had easygoing dispositions, and were even-tempered. Note the similarity to Werner and Smith's (2001) description of their resilient children as attractive to others, socially responsive, active, and easygoing. In both studies, temperament characteristics influenced positive outcomes (social competencies) and ameliorated negative outcomes (behavioral adjustment) for children despite the stressful environments in which they lived.

SUMMARY

Temperament influences the nature and the range of children's experiences as well as the kinds of relationships they have with others. Temperament is understood best within an interactional framework in which both the characteristics of the individual and the characteristics of the context are considered. The concept of goodness of fit is a way to integrate individual and contextual contributions to development and adjustment. Individual differences in children's temperaments serve both active and evocative roles and may be risk or protective influences.

CHAPTER 4

What Is the Basis of Temperament?

Temperament is one of the most important aspects of a child's individuality, behavior, and adjustment. It contributes to children's relationships with others and influences his or her experiences at school and at home. What accounts for these individual differences? What is the basis of temperament? What is the relationship of temperament and intelligence or temperament and personality? How stable is temperament? These questions are discussed in this chapter.

EVIDENCE FOR A BIOLOGICAL BASIS

As noted in Chapter 2, child development experts agree that individual differences in temperament have biological roots. Much of the evidence documenting the biological or constitutional basis of temperament comes from studies of infants or young children. This should come as no surprise, as individual differences in infants' behavior are not adequately explained by their experiences or by socialization effects, given that differences are apparent in the first few weeks after birth. Rather, such differences are more reasonably viewed as biologically based.

Parental Descriptions of Infants

Parents' descriptions of infants' characteristics in the first year—even in the first months of life—are often strikingly different. Some infants are easily aroused, have inconsistent and unpredictable eating and sleeping needs, are irritable and "fussy," and are difficult to soothe. In contrast, other infants seem to self-regulate their eating and sleeping patterns quickly, are easy to soothe, and respond to comforting. Such different responses of infants can be seen in their reactions to a sudden loud noise, such as the sound of a door slamming. One 6-month-old remains calm, turns his head slowly as if interested, and shows no signs of distress. Another has a clear startle response, cries, and is upset. Because these differences are evident very early in infants' lives, it is difficult to attribute them to parenting styles. A more reasonable explanation is that they are biologically based individual differences.

Consistent Research Findings

Questions about the basis of temperament have been addressed by a number of researchers with generally consistent findings. Three examples are illustrative. Rothbart (1989) and her colleagues carried out extensive laboratory studies of temperament in infants and young children, focusing especially on aspects of arousal and self-regulation. Rothbart and Jones have documented individual differences early in infants' activity levels, emotionality, and attention and suggest that these characteristics are ". . . based on a set of brain systems underlying children's reactivity and self-regulation" (1998, p. 479). They suggested that there are differences in the development and timing of these systems such that activation or arousal precedes the emergence of self-regulation. Their findings underscore the importance of considering temperament within a developmental framework.

A second example of biologically based differences in temperament comes from the work of developmental psychologist Jerome Kagan and his associates, who documented individual differences in young children's responses to the unfamiliar (Kagan, Reznik, & Gibbons, 1989). These researchers found that, when faced with something novel or unfamiliar, about 15% of 2- and 3-year-olds were extremely and consistently inhibited; that is, they were shy, quiet, wary, and withdrawing. A different 15% of children were very approaching, socially responsive, and spontaneous. These extreme individual characteristics of inhibition and responsiveness were found to be moderately stable. The differences were not related to intelligence or to social class. Kagan and colleagues documented further that these early extreme behavior characteristics were related to differences in patterns of physiological functions such as heart rate and EEG activation patterns. (See detailed discussions in books edited by Kohnstaam, Bates, and Rothbart, 1989, and Damon, 1998.) Fox, Henderson, Rubin, Calkins, and Schmidt (2001) also focused their work on inhibited and uninhibited children. They referred to the latter as "exuberant." In contrast to their withdrawing and inhibited peers, exuberant children were described as high in sociability, as approaching, and as drawn to novelty. They were not fearful and they were low in distress. Using electrophysiological techniques, these researchers documented differences among groups of inhibited and exuberant infants at age 4 months, finding specifically that the exuberant children had unique EEG (electroencephalogram) patterns. These researchers suggested that there are ". . . . physiological patterns reflecting the disposition toward sociability and approach . . . ." (2001, p. 19) and proposed that the temperament types of consistently inhibited infants are identifiable by characteristic patterns of brain activity.

In summary, there is a large and substantive research literature suggesting that there are biological, neurological, and physiological underpinnings of individual differences in temperament.

Is Temperament Heritable?

Many researchers suggest that temperament is, in part, heritable; that is, that genetics contribute to individual differences in temperament. Though researchers are not in complete agreement about the extent of genetic influence, some consensus exists that temperament traits, especially those for negative attributes such as being prone to fear or anger, are "moderately genetically influenced" (Goldsmith, Lemeny, Aksan, & Buss, 2000, p. 4). This, of course, does not minimize the importance of experience but underscores the need to consider several contributions to individual differences in temperament.

Twins Studies   The findings about heritability have come from comparisons of identical and fraternal twins and assessment of temperament in adoptive and nonadoptive parents and children. The findings from both methods suggest significant heritability, although evidence is stronger from twin studies than from adopted children studies. Two examples are illustrative. Saudino, McGuire, Reiss, Hetherington, and Plomin (1995) analyzed parents' ratings of identical and fraternal twins and their siblings on the Buss and Plomin temperament factors of *easiness, sociability,* and *activity.* They confirmed that heritability was greater for identical than for fraternal twins and greater for twins than for full nontwin siblings, half siblings, and step-siblings. Based on data gathered over the years in the Louisville Twin Study, Matheny (1989) reported significant heritable effects for some, although not all, of the Thomas and Chess (1977) nine temperament dimensions. Genetic contributions were found for activity, approach/withdrawal, persistence, adaptability, and threshold.

The Importance of Experience

The fact that there is a significant genetic component to temperament does not diminish the importance of experience. Indeed, many interesting questions have to do with how these genetic and environmental influences interact to affect development and behavior. DiLalla and Jones (2000) proposed that Gottesman's (1963) "reaction range concept" is useful in thinking about genetic–environment effects on temperament. The idea is that genetic contributions set limits on the range of possible expressions of temperament but that environmental influences affect where in that range the behavior will be expressed. They suggest, for example, that it is unlikely that a child with a genetic predisposition to extreme shyness will become truly extroverted, but that the degree of shyness may be modified through environmental conditions and experience.

> Ramona is a pleasant but quiet 7-year-old whose response to newness is to wait and watch. As a 3-year-old, she was excessively shy and seldom participated in preschool activities. Over the years, she has gained in confidence, and given time, she now interacts with other children in the classroom. She is still described as shy and inhibited compared with other children but is more outgoing and social than in early years.

Similarly, highly active, intense, and reactive children may modulate their behavior over time and situations, but will nonetheless remain in the upper range on these characteristics. A shy and withdrawing child can become more outgoing and social over time when in a classroom with a warm and caring teacher, for example. A very active child can learn to regulate his or her behavior in a supportive classroom in which rules and procedures are well defined.

A reasonable generalization that can be drawn from findings from different research groups is that genetic factors predispose individuals to particular patterns of temperament. This does not suggest that temperament is immutable or that it cannot be modified. Rather, it suggests that how these predispositions become actualized and expressed has to do with development and experience.

TEMPERAMENT AND INTELLIGENCE

Intelligence and temperament are both important dimensions that contribute to the uniqueness of individuals, yet the nature of the relationships between the two is not entirely clear. What is certain, however, is that individual differences in temperament are found within any group of individuals, regardless of whether the individuals have been categorized according to cognitive or intellectual levels. Despite the stereotype that children with Down syndrome are "easy and social," all children with Down syndrome do not have similar temperament profiles. Indeed, some are more accurately described as "difficult," that is, they are withdrawing and negative in mood. Similarly, highly gifted children vary in their behavioral styles, some being approaching and adaptable, others being inhibited and inflexible.

Blair, 10 years old, is an impulsive and high-energy child with Down syndrome. With help and support from his parents and teachers, he has learned to modify somewhat the level of his activity to fit better with environmental demands. Bill, another 10-year-old boy in the same school who also has Down syndrome, is quiet and moody. Teachers work with him on motivation and teamwork.

This common-sense observation is supported by findings from research programs that have addressed the relationship between intelligence and temperament. In most studies, intelligence has been defined as the intelligence quotient (IQ), or with young children as the developmental quotient (DQ). For the most part, IQ, DQ, and temperament are not highly associated, suggesting that each may make somewhat separate contributions to children's learning and development. Matheny (1989) found that correlations between temperament and intelligence were modest and selective; the temperament dimensions of adaptability and attention/persistence were most closely associated with measures of intelligence. Martin, Olejnik, and Gaddis (1994) reported significant correlations between IQ and temperament dimensions of activity, distractibility, and persistence. These findings are in agreement with those in the research of Keogh, Pullis, and Cadwell (1982), who also found only modest associations between intelligence and task orientation.

Differences in the strength of association between temperament characteristics and cognitive ability may be due, in part at least, to the instruments used in assessment and to who does the assessing. In general, teachers' ratings of children's temperament have somewhat stronger correlations with children's tested IQ than do parents' ratings of temperament of the same children. It makes good sense that persistence and low distractibility are relevant to school learning and are especially salient for teachers, whereas other temperament characteristics such as flexibility and adaptability may be more important at home.

The Bi-directional Nature of Intelligence and Temperament

It is unlikely that intelligence and temperament are totally independent. A more reasonable interpretation is that they interact to affect children's behaviors, including those required for success in school. Consider, for example, how the constellation of temperament dimensions making up task orientation influences children's responses to intellectually challenging assignments. Note also that approaching, persistent, and active children engage in a wide range of experiences that contribute to their intellectual competencies. This is not to argue for temperament as a direct contributor to children's intellectual development but to suggest that there are important interactions that affect school learning.

Further, the nature of the interactions between intelligence and temperament are likely bi-directional. That is, cognitive abilities may serve to mediate the expression of temperament, and temperament may influence how intellectual energy is directed and expended. On the one hand, temperament may influence how children approach a school task, the energy they bring to it, and their willingness to "invest" in intellectual activities. On the other hand, intelligence may serve to modify and mediate the expression of temperament. A highly reactive and intense child may modulate her behavior by seeking alternative ways of expressing herself. A temperamentally impulsive, quick-responding child may slow down his actions by telling himself to "cool it."

TEMPERAMENT AND PERSONALITY

One of the continuing debates in temperament work has to do with the relationship between temperament and personality. Certainly there is considerable overlap in the descriptions of each. Comprehensive and detailed reviews of temperament and personality may be found in *The Developing Structure of Temperament from Infancy to Adulthood,* a 1994 publication edited by C.F. Halverson, G.A. Kohnstaam, and R.P. Martin, and in the chapter by Caspi in *The Handbook of Child Psychology* (1998), edited by Damon. For some, temperament is seen as independent of personality; for others, the two are indistinguishable. A reasonable inference is that *personality* is a more inclusive term than *temperament* (Rothbart, 1989) and that temperament is an important component of personality. One of the arguments for differentiating temperament from personality is based on the timing of each. As noted previously, individual differences in temperament are recognizable very early in life, whereas personality emerges over time.

Correspondence Between Temperament and Personality

Temperament dimensions and types have already been described in Chapter 2. Like temperament, personality is described in different ways, but a widely accepted approach identifies the "Big Five" factors: 1) extroversion, 2) agreeableness, 3) conscientiousness, 4) neuroticism, and 5) openness/intellect (Halverson, Kohnstaam, & Martin, 1994).

Prior (1992) pointed out that four of the "Big Five" personality dimensions are similar to temperament dimensions. She suggested that extroversion and approach/withdrawal describe similar characteristics, that agreeableness and positive mood/adaptability/manageability are comparable, that conscientiousness is likened to self-regulation and task orientation, and that neuroticism or emotional stability is similar to mood and intensity of reactions. Caspi (1998) agreed that negative affect and inhibition are likely related to neuroticism and that positive affect and activity may be linked to extroversion and agreeableness. Prior's associations are summarized in Table 4.1.

This is not to imply that inhibited children who are negative in mood will necessarily become neurotic teenagers or adults or that active children with positive affects will become highly extroverted. There are many contributors to personality, and temperamental predispositions are only one. Caspi (1998) suggested that the links between temperament and personality come about through a "process of elaboration" that involves development and experience. These processes include how individual differences in temperament elicit different reactions from those in the environment, how temperament influences the selection of environments and experiences, and how experience is construed or interpreted. From a similar perspective, Goldsmith and colleagues considered that temperamental traits are substrates—that these traits ". . . represent raw material that is modified—and sometimes radically changed to yield the recognizable features of mature human personality" (2000, p. 1).

Table 4.1. Similar dimensions of personality and temperament

Personality	Temperament
Extroversion	Approach/withdrawal
Agreeableness	Positive mood
	Adaptability/manageability
Conscientiousness	Self-regulation
	Task orientation
Neuroticism	Mood
	Intensity of reactions

Source: Prior (1992).

HOW STABLE IS TEMPERAMENT?

One of the major issues with any characteristic of individual differences has to do with stability, and temperament is no exception. There are at least two ways of thinking about consistency or stability: One refers to consistency across different situations; the other refers to stability or continuity over time.

Consistency Across Situations

Although, as noted previously, temperament is evident early on and has roots in biological processes, the expression of temperament is influenced by age, experience, and environment or context. Thus, we should not expect to find one-to-one correspondence among the behavioral expressions of temperament in different situations. Still, highly active people tend to be active in many situations, slow-responding people are predictably slow in responding, and intense people remain intense. In our everyday lives, most of us can describe individuals in ways that allow mutual friends to recognize them. Think of terms used to describe others: "He has a short fuse"; "She never gives up"; "She always takes a negative view"; or "He is constantly on the go." These behavioral descriptors tend to characterize a person in more than one situation, although styles of behaving vary in degree depending on the situation, a point consistent with the concept of "reactive range" referred to previously in this chapter. It is obvious that individuals modify their behavior to meet situational demands, but across many situations there are clear consistencies that characterize them.

Consistency over Time

A second aspect of consistency has to do with stability over time. Certainly, how temperament is expressed is influenced by age, experience, and context. Nonetheless, individuals can be described as having characteristic behavioral styles over time: "He has been energetic from the time he was a child"; "She has always been on the shy side"; or "He was always easy to get along with."

An example of cross-time stability comes from research in the Fullerton Longitudinal Study (Guerin & Gottfried, 1994). These investigators based their work on the Thomas and Chess model, studying the same children over a 10-year period. They found stability for five of the nine Thomas and Chess dimensions from ages 2 to 12; the highest associations were for activity and approach. Associations among temperament dimensions in children from ages 5 to 12 were even stronger; significant correlations were found for all nine dimensions. "Difficultness" in infancy predicted negative mood and low adaptability throughout childhood. Stability across ages was generally similar for boys and girls. Findings in this research are consistent with reports of others who found that continuity varies according to dimensions or clusters studied (Caspi & Silva, 1995).

The specific behavioral expressions of temperament may differ in different developmental periods yet still reflect common underlying predispositions. For example, Fox and colleagues (2001) found that inhibition in infants and young children is often expressed in response to novel objects or people, whereas older children are more likely to be inhibited in new social situations. They refer to the latter as "social reticence" and consider it an age-related expression of behavioral inhibition. They found that early temperament was "modestly predictive" of behavioral reticence at age 4, suggesting some continuity over time. Support for the notion of continuity is not limited to formal research efforts, and everyday examples abound.

Continuity, thus, may be seen in two ways. The actual behaviors may be the same at different times, or the overt behaviors may differ but be expressions of the same underlying temperament.

It should be emphasized that continuity across developmental periods is apt to be stronger when temperament is extreme than when it is mild. Extreme shyness or extreme activity may be modified in response to situational demands and tempered by maturity but will still be characteristic of an individual. The energetic and highly active preschooler will be an active third grader relative to children his or her age. The extremely inhibited elementary school child will be shy compared with other middle school students. Indeed, compared with more moderate expressions of behavioral styles, extreme temperament attributes may be less affected by context and thus appear more stable.

Omar was an outgoing, affectionate, and active 2-year-old who would run up to every newcomer he met. As a 6-year-old, he is always busily involved in school projects and after-school activities. Teachers welcome his enthusiasm and tendency to be the first to raise his hand with answers.

As an example, Kagan, Reznik, and Gibbons (1989) found that about 15% of children in their studies were extremely inhibited or uninhibited when faced with novel or unfamiliar stimuli. Follow-up studies revealed that almost three quarters of the extremely shy and timid preschoolers continued to be inhibited in novel situations at 7 or 8 years of age. The majority of the 2- and 3-year-olds who were considered spontaneous and approaching remained so in the mid-elementary school years. Similar results were found in the Australian (Prior et al., 2000) and New Zealand (Caspi & Silva, 1995) studies, confirming stability over time for those children with extreme temperaments. The New Zealand researchers also reported more continuity of temperament when based on clusters or types rather than on dimensions.

Stability and continuity are influenced by the ways in which temperament is assessed, that is, by the measures used and the ages of those being assessed. This, of course, is not unique to temperament. Infant tests of cognitive/developmental status are heavily weighted with motor items, whereas cognitive tests for older children and adults rely heavily on language. Thus, findings are sometimes different at different ages. Similarly, the specifics of assessing temperament may vary. As is discussed in Chapter 9, there are a number of different methods for assessing temperament, and these techniques tap somewhat different dimensions as well as being appropriate for use at different ages.

> Denise was a highly active and intense 3-year-old who would throw herself on the supermarket floor in a tantrum when told she would not be given candy in the checkout aisle. Now 10 years old, she is often verbally argumentative in similar circumstances when she doesn't get her way.

It is clear that stability, which is closely related, must be viewed in context. Consider how quiet an active, talkative child may be when going to the doctor for his first check-up. Conversely, a quiet and shy teenager may be quite expansive when talking alone with a best friend. Differences between home and school environments also influence the ways that temperament is expressed and how it is interpreted. Particular temperament characteristics such as task orientation, persistence, and distractibility are especially salient in school but less important at home where positive mood and adaptability may have strong affects on family relationships. Not surprisingly, the correlations between parents' and teachers' ratings of children's temperament are moderate at best. Yet, everyday interactions with others provide considerable common-sense evidence that there are differences in behavioral styles that characterize individuals and that these stylistic characteristics are apparent across environments and over time.

SUMMARY

The findings from studies of genetic and biological contributions to temperament document that temperament is in part heritable and that there are biological underpinnings to individual differences. The associations between temperament and intelligence are modest, but temperament and personality have many common components. Considerable evidence argues for moderate stability of temperament over time and across situations. The expression of temperament is affected by development, by experience, and by situational demands, however. Findings to date underscore the importance of considering temperament in an interactional model.

CHAPTER 5

Does Temperament Influence Children's Achievement in School?

Schools are places where, for the first time, children face real and objective standards for success and where they see their achievements relative to the achievements of other children. Preschool children can pretend to "read" a book, but in elementary school, children must really learn to read. Preschoolers can play number games, but elementary school children must learn more advanced arithmetic skills. Children differ greatly in how well and how quickly they master these objective tasks or even whether they can succeed in the traditional sense at all. What accounts for these differences? Intelligence (i.e., cognitive level) is the most frequent reason given for a student's academic success or failure in school, and cognitive ability may be a "necessary but not sufficient" condition for learning. Think of the bright underachieving student or the less cognitively able student who is an outstanding achiever. Although ability is important, it is not the only reason for successful achievement. Prior experiences, motivation, and the quality of instruction all affect student achievement in school. So does temperament.

Chapter 4 contains a brief discussion of how the temperament dimensions of approach, adaptability, and persistence are modestly related to children's IQ scores. These dimensions are also likely contributors to children's achievement in academic subjects. Indeed, it is reasonable that temperament may have an even greater impact on achievement than on intelligence. Students in school must modify and direct their energies and activity levels appropriately and must respond adaptively and flexibly to challenging instructional demands. Students are expected to work on projects that require time and many steps to complete. Some can respond successfully to such demands, others give up early, while others "hang in" until projects are finished. These differences are in part related to individual differences in temperament.

Maggie is a bright 11-year-old with average achievement who does the minimum required to pass. She prefers talking with her friends to doing schoolwork, especially if the assignments are long. She is very sensitive to what is going on around her, often complaining of the temperature of the room, and she spends a great deal of time watching other children or shuffling papers. Both her teachers and her parents are frustrated by her lack of persistence and her distractibility. Sam, in the same class as Maggie, scores in the average range on measures of ability but is consistently in the upper 20% in achievement. He is extremely conscientious, always completing assignments carefully and on time. He works slowly but can concentrate for long periods of time. He is so focused and persistent that he is upset when interrupted.

WHAT DO WE KNOW ABOUT TEMPERAMENT AND ACHIEVEMENT?

Support for the contribution of temperament to children's academic achievement comes from the research of Martin and his associates, who conducted a systematic program of work, focused mainly on preschool and elementary school children (Martin, 1989; Martin, Olejnik, & Gaddis, 1994).

Temperament Characteristics that Influence Learning

Martin and colleagues identified three temperament characteristics as important influences in classroom learning: activity, distractibility, and persistence. Each may contribute positively or negatively to children's success in school.

Activity   Martin described activity as "motoric vigor." Children at the upper extreme cannot seem to sit still, overflow with energy, and have difficulty modulating their activity. Think of the active, fidgety child whose motor seems to run all the time. Quiet time is a problem for this type of child. In contrast, other children are low in energy, tire easily, and prefer quiet time and sedentary activities to physical games. Extremely high or extremely low motoric energy can affect children's behavior in the classroom, contributing to their adjustment and achievement.

Distractibility   Distractibility refers to how easily a child's attention is interrupted by things going on around him or her in the classroom, especially by conditions that are virtually ignored by others. A distractible child has problems staying focused on his or her own seatwork but may attend to noises in the hallway, to the teacher's conversation with another child, and to the whispers of two children in the back of the room.

Persistence   Persistence addresses attention span and the child's ability and willingness to continue working on difficult tasks. Low persistence describes the child who gives up when an assignment is not easily finished, who stops working when the task is hard, and who seems unable to follow through and complete a project. Conversely, other children are overly persistent. They can become so involved in a single activity or school assignment that they are unwilling to stop or change what they are

doing and they become upset when interrupted. Their persistence gets in the way of adapting to the many changing demands
of a classroom. These personal characteristics are well recognized by teachers, and the reasons for the behaviors may be both
motivational and temperamental.

Summary results from five studies in Martin's research program (see Martin, 1989, for a review) are illustrative. In these
studies, children were given standardized achievement tests
anywhere from 5 months to 4 years after teachers rated them on
temperament using Martin's (1988) scale. Findings confirmed
that there were significant negative correlations between activity
level and achievement in reading and math, such that high
activity was associated with low achievement. Associations between distractibility and persistence and reading and math were
even stronger, confirming that children who did not persist well
and who were distractible had lower achievement compared
with their peers.

Especially interesting findings emerged from studies of
temperament and achievement in children as they progressed
through grades one through five. A summary discussion may be
found in Martin, Olejnik, and Gaddis (1994). First-grade teachers' ratings of children's distractibility were correlated negatively with fifth-grade achievement. High persistence in the first
grade was positively associated with achievement in the fifth
grade, suggesting again that persistence is an important attribute in learning success. In contrast, distractibility had a disruptive effect. The magnitude of the associations (the average of correlation coefficients was .41) is impressive given that there was a
4-year time period between ratings of temperament and the assessment of achievement. In these studies, the contribution of intelligence or IQ was taken into account, giving even more weight
to the size of the relationships between temperament and scores
on achievement tests.

The three temperament attributes identified by Martin and
his associates (1994) as important in students' academic achievement are consistent with the findings of temperament research-

ers at the University of California, Los Angeles (UCLA), who also found that the factor of task orientation was significantly related to young children's performance in school (Keogh, 1983, 1989). Findings from both research groups underscored the generalization that temperament dimensions of activity level, distractibility, and persistence, which make up the task orientation factor, have a significant impact on children's learning in school as assessed with standardized achievement measures. This is not surprising given the obvious demands of school for quiet, sustained effort.

The impact of temperament on achievement is not entirely consistent, however, and researchers have found somewhat different patterns of relationships at different ages. For example, Maziade, Coté, Boutin, Boudreault, and Thivierge (1986) reported only minimal relationships between temperament and achievement when the children in their study were 7 years of age, but significant correlations between temperament and achievement when the same children were 12 years old. These findings may reflect differences in children's development and maturity, but they may also be related to differences in the content of instructional programs at different ages. It is likely that temperament characteristics such as persistence and distractibility become increasingly important as the content of the curriculum becomes more complex and assignments become longer and more difficult.

The studies referred to above focused on children in elementary school. An interesting addition comes from the work of Guerin, Gottfried, Oliver, and Thomas (1994), who studied the relationships between temperament and school functioning during early adolescence. This research was part of the Fullerton Longitudinal Study and was based on a sample of more than 100 young adolescents. The findings are particularly relevant to this discussion because the temperament data were gathered from parents (usually the mother) and the school achievement data were based on objective achievement scores gathered from standardized tests of reading and math. As they were with younger students, persistence and distractibility, along with adaptability and predictability, were significantly associated with achievement test scores in reading, and less consistently but significantly with math. These researchers concluded that temperament was related to academic achievement in early adolescence, and like findings in other studies, they confirmed the particular importance of the dimensions of persistence and distractibility.

Achievement and Teachers' Grades

The findings summarized previously were based on standardized tests of achievement. Yet scores on standardized tests are not the only way to measure academic achievement. Because teachers have opportunities to assess children's performance on a day-by-day, hour-by-hour, and even minute-by-minute basis, they have in-depth knowledge about students' performance and problems. Thus, teachers' assigned grades are useful indices of achievement.

As part of their program of research, Martin and Holbrook (1985) examined the relationships between children's temperaments and teachers' grades, finding significant positive associations among the temperament dimensions of adaptability and persistence and teachers' assigned grades in both reading and math. Like Guerin and colleagues' (1994) findings with older students, Martin and Holbrook found that teachers' grades were related to temperament characteristics and that associations between temperament and teachers' ratings of achievement were higher than the correlations between temperament and standardized achievement tests. Findings are summarized in Table 5.1 for reading achievement. Results were similar for achievement in math.

What accounts for the differences in the strength of relationships between temperament and teachers' grades and scores on standardized achievement measures? One possible explanation is that standardized tests provide an "objective" measure of achievement; thus, they are more accurate than are teachers'

Table 5.1. Correlations between temperament dimensions, teachers' grades, and standard achievement test scores for first-grade children

Temperament	Teachers' grades	Standardized tests
Activity	−.43	−.45
Adaptability	.56	.49
Approach/withdrawal	.42	.36
Distractibility	−.56	−.45
Persistence	.65	.49

Source: Martin and Holbrook (1985).

grades. Standardized tests are limited in that they provide only a snapshot of children's performance at one point in time, however, and may underestimate students' achievement, especially for students who are not good "test takers" or for those who were ill or tired on the day of the test. On the one hand, because teachers know their students well, their grades may actually be more accurate indices of achievement. On the other hand, it is possible that because teachers have so many interactions with students, their grading decisions are influenced by students' personal characteristics in addition to their actual levels of achievement—a kind of halo effect at work. As discussed in detail in Chapter 6, considerable agreement exists among teachers about the characteristics they value in students—the personal attributes they think characterize "teachable" students. Many of these characteristics describe individual differences in temperament or behavioral style. In this case, a teacher may subconsciously be inclined to give a particular student a high grade because he works so hard, is task oriented, and is easy to teach. The same teacher may not give the benefit of the doubt to a student perceived as less persistent, as less adaptable, and as more difficult to teach. This, of course, suggests that teachers need to reflect on the basis of their grading decisions in order to ensure equitable treatment of all students.

Whether based on teachers' grades or on standardized tests, considerable evidence exists that individual differences in temperament contribute to children's performance in school. Research reported by Martin, Olejnik, and Gaddis (1994), mentioned earlier in this chapter, is especially relevant and deserves more detailed discussion. Those researchers studied 104 children in six first-grade classes in the same school and documented the importance of task orientation, especially persistence. The majority of the children were in low-income area schools receiving Title 1 funding. In first grade, the children were assessed with a range of tests including Martin's 1988 temperament scale (TABC), and standardized measures of scholastic aptitude and achievement in reading and math. Four years later, the 77 children still in the school were reassessed with standardized achievement tests and teachers' grades at the end of the school year were collected.

Martin et al. proposed a model composed of elements of aptitude, temperament, and first- and fifth-grade achievement to test the predictive power of the early measures and the paths to achievement outcomes. The model was found to explain more than 89% of the variances and co-variances in reading and 94% in math. Teachers' ratings of temperament attributes of level of activity, distractibility, and persistence had three times as much impact on math achievement as did scholastic ability and more than five times that of reading ability. Martin et al. suggested that a plausible interpretation of their findings is that teachers' views of children and their expectations for them affect their behavior and interactions with them, thereby contributing to children's academic self-concept and motivation in school, which in turn affect achievement. Martin and colleagues concluded, "Whatever the causal mechanism, this research indicates that one set of temperament characteristics makes a substantial contribution to the prediction of academic achievement on short- and long-term bases" (1994, p. 67). One can speculate that temperament may be useful in programs aimed at early identification of children at risk for low school achievement.

Pullis and Cadwell (1982) also found that teachers' views of children's temperaments, especially their views of children's task orientation, played a significant part in their classroom management decisions. This study was based on teachers' ratings of

321 elementary school children. Similar results documenting the contributions of task orientation were reported in the University of California, Los Angeles, studies of preschoolers and children with learning disabilities (see Keogh, 1989, for discussion). Findings from these studies are important, as Carey and McDevitt (1995) estimated that approximately 10%–20% of children in any school population are low in task orientation. They suggested that this figure applies across cognitive levels and socioeconomic conditions. On a day-to-day basis, then, teachers must deal with children who bring different temperaments to the classroom. Children who are able to moderate their activity, who can focus and persist, and who can minimize distractions fit well with instructional and behavioral demands. Temperament patterns of other children may be less compatible and present challenges to teachers as well as contribute to achievement.

HOW DOES TEMPERAMENT CONTRIBUTE TO ACHIEVEMENT?

Relationships between children's academic achievement and temperament, particularly the temperament characteristics making up task orientation, have been documented. An important question has to do with *how* temperament contributes to performance in school. Several explanations are plausible, some having to do with direct effects of temperament on children's behavior, others suggesting more indirect contributions to achievement.

Direct Effects on Learning

Considering direct effects on learning, as noted previously, individual differences in temperament influence the vigor and enthusiasm students bring to new learning. Surely the child who approaches learning tasks with enthusiasm, who persists, who moderates activity, who minimizes distractions, and who adapts to changes in format and content has a good probability of success. Conversely, the child who is inhibited, who is put off by new demands, and who is slow to adapt or the child who has difficulty regulating activity level, who is easily distracted, and who does not persist on tasks presents challenges.

Maya, a 9-year-old, thrives in her classroom, which is alive with activity. She is high in approach and energy and is very social, attracted to novelty and change. Occasionally she is too exuberant, but she settles down quickly when the teacher speaks to her about it.

Children may be similar in cognitive ability but may differ dramatically in how they respond to the demands of school. Consider the differences in exploratory behavior between inhibited and uninhibited children, or the range of experiences of shy or exuberant children. Think about how these individual differences in behavioral styles affect the nature of everyday activities in school. Some children like change, find new assignments interesting and challenging, and are persistent and task involved, leading them toward more opportunities for learning compared with their peers. These characteristics are likely influences on achievement.

Individual differences in children's temperaments also contribute to the goodness of fit between students and other aspects of the education program. A child may not perform well in the classroom for a number of reasons—a mismatch or lack of "fit" between the level of instruction and the child's ability, interest, motivation, and temperament. All contribute to successful or not-so-successful learning. Consider, too, the context of classrooms in which instruction occurs. A visit to any school reveals that classrooms differ in the organization of space and in the content and methods of instruction. Classrooms also differ in affective tone, with some providing a relaxed, warm, and friendly atmosphere for children while others are less accepting, more competitive, and less supportive.

In many classrooms there are 25 or more children engaged in many ongoing activities. Yet, children are expected to sit quietly, to pay attention, to follow directions from the teacher, and "to keep their hands to themselves." Children are also expected to move efficiently from assignment to assignment, and to deal with transitions and changes in demands. For many children, these tasks are accomplished easily, but for some the requirements of classroom behavior may be difficult to meet and their learning is disrupted.

It is likely that particular constellations of temperament may be differentially important and have different functional significance depending on the nature of the classroom. A classroom in which routines are highly structured and only a limited range of behaviors are tolerated may fit well with some children's behavioral styles but may be less compatible with others. A crowded, busy, and unstructured classroom may be optimal for particular children but overwhelming for others. The distractible elementary school child who is slow to warm up or the intense and highly reactive child may find a crowded, busy classroom upsetting.

Two of Caspi and Silva's (1995) clusters of New Zealand children, who were described in Chapter 2 of this book, illustrated differences in behavioral styles that seem likely to interact with classroom routines and affect learning and achievement. The undercontrolled children were described as having trouble sitting still, as being rough and uncontrolled in their behavior, and as labile in their emotional responses. The confident children were described as approaching; they were ". . . willing and eager to tackle and explore . . . and seemed to adjust to the new circumstances very quickly" (1995, p. 489). These differences in behavioral styles have consequences for how children succeed in school because they affect children's involvement with the content of instruction, with peers, and with teachers.

> Jeremy finds a high-activity classroom overwhelming. He is a quiet and slow-to-warm-up child who is uncomfortable with change. He likes order and a regular routine, and he needs time to adapt to something new. His response to the many activities in the classroom is to withdraw and work diligently on a specific assignment. The other children like him but for the most part leave him alone.

Rothbart and Jones (1998) made another important point about individual differences in temperament and school classrooms. They noted that temperament affects the ways children experience what is thought to be a common environment. In other words, while structurally and physically the same, a given classroom is not the same for all students in it. Children with low sensory thresholds are especially sensitive to the physical environment, to noise, to extraneous activity in a classroom, even to the temperature of the classroom. As in the cafeteria at lunchtime, such children may be easily overwhelmed by too much stimulation and may be uncomfortable and have difficulty completing academic assignments. In contrast, other children may be overly excited by the same situation. They may quickly become out of control, engaging in behaviors that disrupt their attention to task and disturb other students. Though physically the classroom "looks" the same to all children, those of different temperaments experience it in different ways.

Kai also finds a high-activity classroom difficult. He is an intense and reactive "prickly" boy who is easily out of control. Because the classroom is so free flowing, he often intrudes on other children, which leads to unpleasant and sometimes even aggressive verbal interchanges. He thinks the other children do not like him and he is correct. They find him negative, demanding, and disruptive.

The findings about temperament and achievement also underscore the importance of attention in school learning. Much of what happens in school requires flexible and selective attention and effortful control. These refer to the ability to sustain one activity at the expense of another and the ability to modulate or change attention and behavior in response to instructional demands. Individual differences in temperament may influence children's effortful control and affect their classroom habits and learning (Rothbart & Jones, 1998). Specific aspects of effortful control include how efficiently students can switch from one activity to another and how effective students are in persisting on academic assignments and modulating their activities to meet task and situational demands. Goldsmith, Lemeny, Aksan, and Buss also underscored the importance of "... attentional processes and ability to intentionally inhibit ongoing behaviors" (2000, p. 3) in children's adjustment. The idea that attention is critical to learning is not new, but linking attentional characteristics to temperament may provide a fresh way to consider problems in school learning.

Finally, Guerin and colleagues (1994) identified significant associations between temperament and achievement but found also that temperament was associated with the social/behavioral demands of school. In the work of Guerin and associates, parents' ratings of their children's predictability, persistence, adaptability, and negative mood were significantly associated with teachers' ratings of valued classroom behaviors such as "working hard" and "behaving appropriately." It is likely that working hard and behaving appropriately affect teachers' views of students and how they respond to them, as well as affecting how children deal with learning tasks. A reasonable inference is that temperament contributes to how children's behavior in school mediates learning success by focusing or disrupting attention to task and by influencing teachers' perceptions of their abilities and achievements. Thus, temperament may make both direct and indirect contributions to achievement.

Indirect Effects of Temperament on Achievement

Classrooms are social places, and most instruction is embedded in social interchanges between students, teachers, and peers, interchanges that are related in part to individual differences in temperament. The nature of these interactions have consequences for students' behavior and achievement. They also have consequences for students' views of their own academic competencies and problems. As noted earlier, performance in school is very public, and the level of a child's achievement on academic tasks is well recognized by other students, the social context re-inforcing the impact of success or failure on children's own views of themselves.

Direct effects of temperament attributes such as distractibil-ity and lack of persistence on achievement have already been de-scribed. Individual differences in temperament may also have indirect effects on educational outcomes. Indirect effects on achievement are illustrated in Martin's (1988) model in which he proposed a number of "intermediate steps" between children's temperament and achievement outcomes. Figure 5.1 describes how both home and school effects converge to influence school outcomes, although the discussion here is focused only on school effects.

As shown in Figure 5.1, Martin described an indirect path-way between temperament and educational outcomes. He sug-gested that the contribution of individual differences in chil-dren's temperament is mediated by the attitudes and responses of teachers and peers and that these, in turn, contribute to the academic self-concept of the child, leading to differences in schooling outcomes. The model identifies relationships between students' temperaments and teachers' attitudes, instructional decisions, and behavior—points to be elaborated in Chapter 6. The model also describes relationships between temperament characteristics and the attitudes and behavior of peers that affect how children see themselves. Note that the arrows between the components of the model point in two directions, underscoring the interactional nature of the relationships. Although educa-tional outcome are targeted, the same model may reasonably be applied to outcomes regarding behavioral and social adjust-ment. The model provides a useful way to think about tempera-ment in the context of school and underscores the point that tem-perament can have indirect, long-term effects on achievement.

Caspi and Silva (1995) illustrated the long-term impact of individual–environmental interactions when they proposed the concept of *cumulative continuity,* which describes how individual differences have consequences that may accumulate

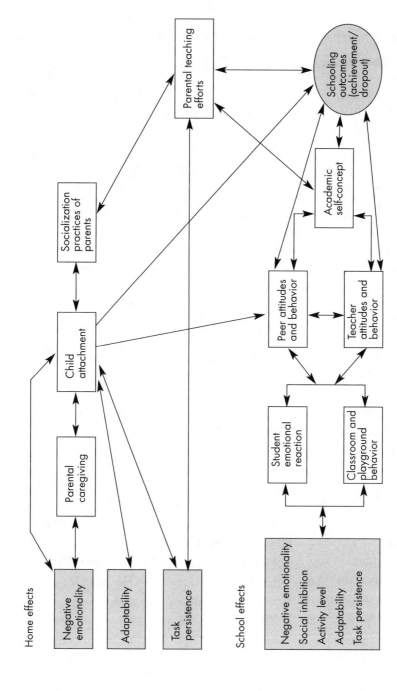

Figure 5.1. Home and school effects on a child's temperament interact with one another and eventually converge to influence schooling outcomes for the child. (From Martin, R.P. [1992]. Child temperament effects on special education: Process and outcomes. *Exceptionality, 3,* p. 109; reprinted by permission.)

Home effects

- Negative emotionality
- Adaptability
- Task persistence

Parental caregiving

Child attachment

Socialization practices of parents

Parental teaching efforts

School effects

- Negative emotionality
- Social inhibition
- Activity level
- Adaptability
- Task persistence

Student emotional reaction

Classroom and playground behavior

Peer attitudes and behavior

Teacher attitudes and behavior

Academic self-concept

Schooling outcomes (achievement/dropout)

and be elaborated over time. They noted, for example, that impulsive and undercontrolled children who have problems conforming in school might receive less instruction than their more adaptable and conforming peers. Students who do not fit the behavioral and academic requirements of school are also apt to have unsatisfactory interactions with teachers and to spend considerable time in noninstructional situations; for example, they might spend more time in "time-out," in visits to the principal's office, or in talking with the school counselors. The cumulative impact over time can lead to less satisfactory skills, which then affect subsequent achievement and adjustment. Temperament, thus, may have both short- and long-term effects.

SUMMARY

Considerable evidence documents relationships between children's temperament and their achievement in school. Some inconsistencies in patterns and strength of relationships can be found among different research groups, in what achievement domains are considered, and in how achievement is assessed. Researchers concur, however, that temperament does influence school performance. Children's temperaments may affect their success in school in several ways, such as how they approach, become involved in, and persist in learning tasks; their behaviors in the classroom; and how teachers respond to them. The temperament dimensions of activity, persistence, and distractibility that make up a broader factor of task orientation are especially important contributors to children's achievement and behavior. These dimensions appear to have real functional significance in school classrooms and to exert both direct and indirect influence on children's academic behaviors.

CHAPTER 6

Does Temperament Influence Teachers' Academic Decisions?

Teaching is not just a matter of ladling out information, of providing bite-sized chunks of knowledge for students to consume. Rather, teachers are decision makers—day by day, minute by minute, teachers make decisions about individual children in terms of academic tasks: What should I focus on in the reading or spelling assignment? Who should be called on to read aloud? How much time should students have to finish a math assignment? What should students do when they finish an assignment? Teachers also make many decisions about behavior management: Should a student be given a verbal cue or a reprimand? Should I ignore troublesome behavior or respond to it? Should I move a child to another part of the room? Should I allow a child to move around the room?

Teachers make hundreds of decisions each day, and these decisions are not random. Rather, they are based on teachers' views of children; on the ways teachers synthesize or integrate information about individual students and groups of students. This information includes teachers' perceptions of students' cognitive abilities, competencies in the subject matter being taught, and interests and motivations. Teachers' decisions are also influenced by their own beliefs and values, their preconceived ideas about what students *should* be like, expectations about behavior and achievement, and the nature of their personal interactions with students. Chapter 5 focused on temperament and students' achievement in school, including how individual differences in students' temperaments contribute to their performance on standardized tests and to teachers' assigned grades. This chapter looks at the importance and influence of students' temperament on teachers' perceptions, expectations, and behaviors, including their decisions about how to work with students.

> Mrs. Andrews shakes her head when she looks at Will, a low-energy, inhibited boy who is generally nonresponsive or negative. She feels that Will "could do better if he would only try." She has become increasingly frustrated, critical, and short-tempered with him, and their interactions are stressful at best. Another student, Jennie, is also inhibited and quiet, but she smiles and looks engagingly at the teacher even though she rarely knows the answers to questions. Mrs. Andrews attributes Jennie's poor achievement to limited ability and works hard at modifying Jennie's assignments to ensure her success.

RESEARCH ON TEACHERS' PERCEPTIONS AND EXPECTATIONS

Before discussing evidence that links children's temperament to teachers' behavior, some of the research on teachers' expectations is addressed. For years, a number of researchers have argued that teachers' interactions with individual students are determined, in part, by the expectations they hold for them. For example, Stipek stated, "Expectations affect the content and pace of the curriculum, the organization of instruction, evaluation, instructional interactions with individual students, and many subtle and not-so-subtle messages that affect students' own expectations for learning, and thus, their behaviors" (1998, p. 203).

Teachers' attitudes and expectations are influenced by characteristics of the students they teach. Educators expect higher levels of academic achievement from exceptionally capable children than from those who struggle with learning assignments. They may also have different expectations for particular students or groups of students. These differences, in turn, lead to different decisions about instruction and management strategies. A possible problem, of course, is that these expectations may result in inappropriate or inadequate instruction for whole groups of children based on gender, social class, or ethnicity. Expectations may be expressed in many ways: "Children from poor families lack motivation"; "Girls are not good at math"; or "Parents from ethnic minorities don't value education." These views may also be applied to individual children based on prior experiences with a child or with the siblings or family: "I've taught that kid before; he won't try to learn"; "He is trouble, just like his brother"; or "Her mother is pushy and interfering." Often, teachers' expectations for students' behavior and how they see their potential for

Marta is a shy and slow-to-warm-up 6-year-old. The first 2 months of first grade were painful for her and she watched the other children rather than interact with them. She spoke very quietly in an almost inaudible voice. She worked on assignments slowly and carefully but often did not finish on time. Not surprising, Ms. Medici, the teacher, seldom called on her. After a few months, Marta made some friends, adapted to the routines of the classroom, and was increasingly comfortable in school. According to Mrs. Medici, Marta has begun to "bloom." She participates more enthusiastically and the level of her school work improved greatly. Mrs. Medici's expectations for Marta have also changed, as has the amount of time and attention she gives her.

achievement start early on in the school year and build up over time. Slow-to-warm-up children may have problems adjusting in the first few months of school, setting the stage for a teacher to doubt their abilities or motivations; these doubts can lead to subsequent decisions about instruction.

The important point is that expectations influence teachers' decisions and behaviors, such that teachers treat individual children or groups of children differently. As has been stated many times in this book, life in the classroom is not the same for all students. Some receive positive attention from teachers. Some have mostly negative or punitive interactions with teachers. This, in turn, may lead students to react differently, thus reinforcing the teachers' initial expectations. Take, for example, the interesting and controversial work of Rosenthal and Jacobson in their 1968 book, *Pygmalion in the Classroom*. In this study, Rosenthal and Jacobson told teachers that some students in their classroom had high potential for academic growth. In fact, the children had been identified randomly and the information was without basis. When the students were assessed 8 months later, the randomly selected "high potential" students had made greater cognitive gains than had the non-identified students in the same classrooms, leading to the notion of a "self-fulfilling prophecy" based on teachers' expectations. The Rosenthal and Jacobson study has been criticized on methodological grounds, but the findings are consistent with a large body of research that underscores the impact of teachers' expectations on their interactions with students and on students' performance in school.

Stipek (1998) summarized findings from a number of different researchers to show that teachers have different expectations for and interact differently with high and low-achieving students. She pointed out, for example, that teachers grant more privileges to high achievers than to poor achievers, and that high achievers receive more opportunities for learning, including being called on more often. These differences in teachers' behaviors can influence the students' own self-perceptions, so it should not come as a surprise that poor achievers' confidence in their own abilities decreases over time. In general, the gap between high and poor achievers gets larger as students move up the grades in school.

Stipek argued that teachers need to be aware of how their expectations affect students' learning and achievement and offered implicit and explicit suggestions for communicating high expectations to all students: by expressing their confidence that students can perform well, encouraging persistence to tasks, providing appropriately challenging assignments, maintaining high standards for all students, and ensuring that all students receive attention. She suggested, too, that teachers regularly re-examine their judgments about individual students and review their assumptions about why students behave as they do because these assumptions are the basis for instructional decisions. This kind of reflection may be especially helpful when teachers are faced with children with very different temperaments, as temperamental differences are likely contributors to teachers' expectations for children's achievement and behavior.

Teachers' beliefs and their expectations for individual students and groups of students often go unrecognized but must be considered part of the classroom ecology, as they affect teachers' relationships with students as well as their instructional decisions. Teachers' expectations are only part of the picture, however. Children bring a whole range of personal characteristics, including temperament, to the classroom. These different student characteristics match or don't match teachers' expectations, leading to a "good" or a "not so good" fit. Classroom life is likely to be smooth and positive when children's characteristics are compatible with teachers' expectations. The experiences of both students and teachers are apt to be stressful when the fit is not good.

The Impact of Students' Temperament on Teachers' Decisions

Individual differences in students' aptitudes have long been recognized as important in school. Less attention has been paid to the impact of temperament or behavioral styles on students' and teachers' experiences in the classroom. As noted previously, differences in behavioral styles affect teachers' decisions and behaviors and the ways they work with students. Most teachers agree that highly active, impulsive, and intense children can disrupt routines and lead to stressful encounters in even the best-planned classrooms. Most teachers also agree that inhibited and withdrawing children present different, but nonetheless just as important, challenges.

Research on Teachers' Attitudes

Several programs of research add to the understanding of temperament influences on teachers' perceptions and behaviors. A few selected studies are illustrative:

A number of years ago, Silberman (1969) found that teachers' attitudes toward individual students could fit into four categories: attachment, concern, rejection, and indifference. Silberman posed four questions to teachers to measure these attitudes, paraphrased as follows:

1. If you could keep one child in your room for another year because he or she is such a pleasure to work with, who would it be?
2. Who is the student you are most concerned about?
3. If the principal came to your room and said one child could be moved to another classroom, whom would you choose?
4. If a parent came unexpectedly for a conference, which student would you be least prepared to talk about?

Silberman found that teachers' behaviors and interactions with individual students differed according to which of the four attitudes—attachment, concern, rejection, and indifference—the teacher expressed toward the child as reflected in these questions. The children who were evaluated positively fell in the attachment group and teachers responded to their requests for help. The children whom the teachers were concerned about had the most contact with teachers, while the group of children the teachers seemed indifferent to received the least contact. The children in the rejection group had frequent—but primarily negative—interactions with teachers.

In subsequent work, Martin, Nagle, and Paget (1983) asked teachers to identify children who fit each of the Silberman groups. Teachers also described the children's temperaments using Martin's temperament scale. Next, the patterns of temperaments of the children in the four groups were compared. Children in the attachment group were viewed as more adaptable, more approaching, and more persistent. Children in the indifferent group were described as less active, less approaching, and less intense. The rejection group was different from the three other groups in that the children were more active and more distractible. The concern group children did not differ from the others in temperament.

The temperament patterns of these first graders in Martin's study were consistent with the earlier Silberman work and with the findings from the program of research from the UCLA program. For example, in one UCLA study (a large vignette study), Keogh, Yoshioka-Maxwell, Cadwell, Wilcoxen, and Wright (1982) found that children's temperaments, especially as they related to task orientation, had a major impact on teachers' decisions about supervision, readiness, potential, and special needs. Recall that task orientation is composed of the temperament dimensions of persistence, distractibility, and activity. These dimensions make sense in terms of the demands of school. The skills of being able to modify activity, to attend to instructions, and to persist on assignments facilitate learning and are valued by teachers. Unfortunately, not all students bring these characteristics to the classroom. It is no surprise that children who are highly active, distractible, and low in persistence present problems for teachers.

The UCLA research documented that teachers' perceptions and expectations were influenced by individual differences in students' temperaments and that these perceptions and expectations were translated into instructional and management decisions. Temperament factors of reactivity and adaptability were found to be especially important influences on teachers' decisions in social and management areas. Compared with children with positive temperaments, children with negative temperament patterns were seen by teachers as requiring more supervision and direction. In general, teachers rated girls higher than boys on task orientation and rated children from the least advantaged socioeconomic backgrounds lower than their middle-income peers. Another interesting finding was that teachers rated children with positive temperament profiles as more intelligent than those with negative profiles.

In further work, Pullis and Cadwell (1982) tested the notion that children's temperaments influenced teachers' decisions. They did so by asking teachers to rate their students' temperaments, to estimate their general ability or intelligence, their motivation, their social skills, their academic performance, and whether they worked up to potential. Teachers were also asked how much they would have to monitor a child's behavior in five classroom situations: independent seatwork, small-group activities requiring sharing, academic transitions, transitions from outside to the classroom, and free play in class. Findings confirmed that the temperament attributes making up task orientation were highly correlated with teachers' ratings of children's motivation, academic performance, and potential, but less so with estimates of ability. Task orientation was consistently the most important influence on teachers' decisions across all classroom situations, a finding confirmed by Pullis (1985) in research with mainstream and resource room teachers. Clearly, teachers were responding to differences in children's behavioral styles when making their decisions.

Taken as a whole, these findings provide support for the salience of temperament as an individual difference important in teachers' perceptions of students and in the nature of the fit between teacher and child. A reasonable inference is that children's behavioral styles that are consistent with teachers' expectations have a good probability of leading to compatible and positive experiences in the classroom for both students and teachers. This notion was examined in studies of temperament and teachability.

Temperament and Teachability

In any classroom, some students seem to fit nicely with the teacher's ideas of what a student "should" be like. Conversely, there are also students whose personal characteristics and behaviors are discrepant from the teacher's views and expectations. This idea is, of course, closely linked to the notion of goodness of fit. A good fit results when children have personal attributes and characteristics that are compatible with the teachers' views of what makes students "teachable." For example, Wentzel found that teachers preferred students who are "cooperative, cautious, and responsible" more than they preferred those who are "independent, assertive, and disruptive" (1996, p. 217).

The notion that teachers hold well-defined ideas about students' teachability was studied by Kornblau (1982), who found that teachers have consistent views about the attributes or personal characteristics of teachable students. As part of her research, teachers generated a list of approximately 300 adjectives describing an "ideal" student. These descriptors were the basis of the Teachable Pupil Survey, a 33-item scale made up of three primary dimensions: Cognitive–Motivational Behaviors, School-Appropriate Behaviors, and Personal–Social Behaviors. Two other characteristics received strong endorsement from teachers but were not included in the three primary dimensions: 1) being cooperative and 2) being adaptable to changing classroom routines.

The Cognitive–Motivational descriptors receiving almost unanimous support from teachers included such items as "bright," "clear-thinking," "logical," "curious," "imaginative," and "enterprising." Descriptors in the School-Appropriate Behaviors dimension included the following: "begins and completes classroom tasks," "completes work on time," "alert," "sensitive to classroom procedures," "eager and enthusiastic about classroom activities," and "willingly participates in classroom activities." The Personal–Social attributes highly valued by teachers included the following: "calm, confident, empathetic, happy, cheerful, [and] outgoing." Many of the descriptors are reminiscent of temperament attributes or children's behavioral styles, suggesting that students' temperaments—especially adaptability, persistence, approach, and positive mood—are important to teachers. Characteristics of teachable students as described by teachers in the study are summarized in Table 6.1.

The role of temperament in teachers' views was demonstrated also in research linking students' temperaments to teachers' ratings of students' teachability (Keogh, 1982, 1994; Kornblau & Keogh, 1980). Students rated high on teachability had positive temperament profiles, with factors of task orientation and adaptability listed as most important. In contrast, those who were low in task orientation and personal–social flexibility were considered less teachable. The importance of task orientation in teachers' views of teachability was documented further in a study of children with learning disabilities in which students' temperaments were found to be more strongly associated with teachers' ratings of teachability than were the students' cognitive abilities (Keogh, 1983). Note that the temperament configuration of poor adaptability and high distractibility is consistent with Thomas and Chess's (1977) description of difficult children.

Thus, evidence supports the notion that teachers bring ideas about what students "should" be like to the classroom and that these ideas influence their perceptions of and expectations for individual students. Such preconceptions also influence teachers' behaviors and interactions with students. A visit to any classroom demonstrates that teachers' attention and instructional efforts are not spread equally among all children in the classroom; some receive far more attention than others. Important to note, too, is that the nature of teachers' interactions with

Table 6.1.   Teachers' views of characteristics of teachable pupils

Dimension X: Cognitive–motivational behaviors

bright (100%)
clear-thinking, logical, rational (95%)
curious, inquisitive, questioning (80%)
enterprising, inventive in thinking (75%)
high verbal ability (90%)
intelligent (95%)
imaginative, uses materials in an original manner (80%)
insightful, perceptive (75%)

Dimension Y: School-appropriate behaviors

able to begin and complete classroom tasks (100%)
academic achievement appropriate for age and grade (75%)
alert, attentive to classroom proceedings (100%)
attention span appropriate for age and grade (90%)
completes work on time (95%)
eager, enthusiastic about classroom activities (85%)
enjoys school work (95%)
follows directions (100%)
willingly participates in classroom activities (85%)

Dimension Z: Personal–social behaviors

calm (100%)
confident (90%)
considerate to others (100%)
emotionally stable (100%)
empathetic, understanding of feelings of others (100%)
extroverted, outgoing (100%)
friendly (100%)
happy, cheerful (100%)
has sense of humor (100%)
honest (100%)
pleasant, good-natured (100%)
sincere (100%)
socially well-adjusted (95%)
well-accepted and liked by peers (95%)

Miscellaneous

cooperative (70%-Z; 30%-Y)
adaptable to changing classroom routines (60%-Y; 40%-Z)

different students varies. With some children, teachers engage in many friendly, "fun" exchanges. With others, especially those students viewed as low in teachability, the interactions are apt to be primarily managerial and instructional, with few social exchanges. A reasonable inference is that teachers' behaviors are influenced by their views and expectations about students' teachability and that these views are, in part at least, related to individual differences in children's temperaments.

The relationships between temperament and teachability were examined further in work by UCLA researchers (Keogh, 1994) in a study of 360 children who were in four different school placements: 1) general elementary school, 2) general preschool, 3) special education elementary school, and 4) special education preschool. The groups were found to differ on teachers' ratings on the three temperament factors of task orientation, personal–social flexibility/adaptability, and reactivity. All teacher rating differences were found in favor of general education students over the special education groups, and girls over boys. The groups also differed on the teachers' ratings on all three of the teachability factors of cognitive–motivational characteristics, school-appropriate behaviors, and personal–social skills. Girls were viewed more favorably than boys on school-appropriate behaviors and personal–social skills. For all groups the strongest associations between temperament and teachability were for task orientation and school-appropriate behaviors. Significant associations were also found between the temperament reactivity factor, especially dimen-

Theresa thrives in first grade. She learns quickly and responds enthusiastically to new opportunities and experiences. She loves going on field trips and is also diligent about meeting the teacher's high standards. Theresa is often given responsibilities such as line leader and attendance checker. Her teacher, Mr. Miller, has already assigned her to the highest reading group and is encouraging her to try out for the lead in the class's play. Mr. Miller has said more than once that if all students were like Theresa, teaching would be "a snap."

sions of mood and intensity, and teachers' views of children's personal/social competencies.

In further work by UCLA researchers, teachers' ratings of an "ideal" student were compared with their ratings of actual children, making it possible to derive a discrepancy score for each child. Children with negative discrepancy scores were low on temperament factors of task orientation and personal/social flexibility and were high on reactivity. Based on their findings, UCLA researchers concluded that temperament and teachability are not synonymous, but that both are important ingredients in the teacher–student mix. The notion of teachability is broader and more encompassing than temperament, but individual differences in children's temperament are significant contributors to teachers' views of teachability.

Temperament–Expectation Interactions

How do children's temperaments and teachers' expectations and perceptions interact? The notion of goodness of fit is relevant here. We can speculate that there will be a poor fit when a child's behavioral style is discrepant from a teacher's views of what makes a child "teachable." We can also speculate that teachers differ in how they perceive and interpret individual differences in children's temperaments. Some teachers value intense, energetic, and active children because they perceive them as enthusiastic, spirited, and involved. Other teachers find the same children difficult to teach. Some teachers work well with quiet, shy, and withdrawing children; others find them uninvolved and unresponsive. A possible consequence of a discrepancy between teachers' views and children's temperament is that the teachers' decisions about instruction and management may be inappropriate and even ineffective.

As noted earlier, teachers may make different attributions about the reasons for children's behaviors. We all make inferences about the causes of our own behaviors and about the behaviors of others: "I failed the geography test because I didn't study"; "She did well on the math test because she is smart"; "She doesn't do well because she doesn't like to work hard"; or, "He misbehaves on purpose to annoy me." Interestingly, most of the time we don't ask about the reasons for children's behavior when the behavior is compatible with what we want and expect. We make attributions about causes when the behavior is discrepant with our expectations, however. (See Weiner, 1992, for discussion of attribution theory.)

An important point is that teachers' decisions about how to respond to differences in students' behaviors will vary, in part, according to the attributions teachers make about the reasons for the behavior. Think of the different ways a teacher might respond depending on whether a child's active, intense, and intrusive behavior is viewed as purposefully disruptive or as temperament-based exuberance? Misbehavior viewed as purposefully annoying is apt to evoke negative, punitive reactions, while behaviors viewed as part of a child's behavioral style are more easily tolerated. This concept can be seen in ways a teacher might interpret a child's unwillingness to take on a new assignment. Is the response due to poor motivation, laziness, limited ability, or an inhibited behavioral style that makes the student reluctant and withdrawing when faced with changes and new demands? Teachers' interpretations of withdrawing behavior influence their responses, sometimes leading to changes in the instructional task, sometimes to encouragement and help, or possibly to negative or punitive actions.

Sensitivity to individual differences in children's temperament is an important attribute for an educator to have, and thinking about children's behavior as temperament-related can change the ways teachers interpret behaviors. Recognizing that many classroom behaviors are temperament based, rather than motivationally based, may "take the edge off" what otherwise might be a disruptive relationship between teacher and child. Viewing a child's behavior as stylistic rather than deliberate makes it easier to accept and to deal with positively.

SUMMARY

Teachers are engaged in hundreds of ongoing instructional and management decisions about students every day. These decisions are influenced by teachers' beliefs about what students should be like as well as by individual characteristics of children or groups of children. Teachers' expectations about students are captured in the notion of teachability, and temperament is one of the contributors to teachers' views. Positive interactions are likely when there is a good fit between teachers' expectations and children's attributes, but negative interactions are often the product of a poor fit.

CHAPTER 7

Are Temperament and Behavior Problems Related?

Teachers frequently voice their concerns about how to work with children with behavior and adjustment problems. Problem behaviors in the classroom range from occasional acts of mild disobedience to persistent defiance and aggression to violent outbursts. The recent tragic examples of school shootings are sobering reminders of the seriousness of problems that teachers may encounter. Fortunately, such extreme behavior is rare, but verbal aggression and serious challenges to teachers' authority occur almost daily. These behaviors result in disruptions in the classroom that affect other students as well as the teacher and take time and attention away from the instructional program.

It is important to note that teachers are also faced with extremely anxious and withdrawn children and with those who are socially isolated, hypersensitive, and easily hurt and upset. Because acting out behaviors disrupt classroom routines and instruction, students who act out typically receive a great deal of attention; but excessively withdrawn children have special needs, too. Responding to the range of behaviors in any classroom is a complex and difficult task.

Behavior problems may have many causes and many expressions. Some problems are situationally specific, evident only at home or at school or in the classroom or on the playground. Behavior problems may occur primarily when a child is in a particular situation in the classroom, when seated with certain other children, during long instructional periods, when expected to work on certain subjects, or when faced with a particularly difficult assignment. Similarly, children may withdraw and cease to try in situations when they feel stressed and threatened by other children or classroom demands.

In contrast, other problem behaviors may be chronic and pervasive and evident at home, in the classroom, and on the playground. Such problems may be evidence of an underlying psychopathology that requires major intervention and treatment. Particularly troublesome are conduct disorders involving bullying, destroying property, lying and stealing, and aggression toward others. Forness, Kavale, and Walker defined *conduct disorder* as "a term often used by school professionals for children with intractable antisocial behavior; as a psychiatric diagnosis it is characterized by a repetitive or persistent pattern of behavior violating basic rights of others . . . or major norms or rules" (1999, p. 138). They noted further that conduct disorders are seen in as many as 4%–10% of children and adolescents, although fortunately, the behaviors may be only mild or moderate. It is important to emphasize that conduct problems described by Forness et al. differ in severity and persistence from classroom problems that are based on the interactions between individual differences in children's temperaments and the demands and routines of school.

Nonetheless, in any classroom there may be children who present challenges to teachers' authority and who disrupt classroom environments. Indeed, teachers often complain that their opportunities to teach are minimized because their time and energies are taken up with behavior management, with control problems, and with the demands of a few children. A common complaint is "I spend all my time with three or four kids." Certainly, real differences exist among classrooms in how much time is spent in teaching and how much time is spent in managing, and management becomes the issue when a child with a serious conduct problem is present. Most problems are not extreme, however, and reflect both the characteristics of the students as well as the ways classrooms and instructional programs are organized and implemented. As noted in Chapter 6, they also reflect the expectations and behaviors of the teachers. The "fit" among these determines, in part at least, the nature of the classroom environment and how teachers' time and energies are used.

WHAT DO WE KNOW ABOUT BEHAVIOR PROBLEMS?

Before considering the role of temperament in behavior problems, it is instructive to briefly discuss behavior problems themselves. The usual approach to understanding children's behavior problems is to focus on the children in order to determine "what is the matter with them" that accounts for their behavior. Psychologists and psychiatrists have a whole armamentarium of tests and techniques to assess and document children's problem behaviors, and a large clinical literature documents a range of specific problems. Two major dimensions of problems, externalizing and internalizing, emerge consistently. *Externalizing* problems are those involving aggressive, acting out, disruptive behaviors. *Internalizing* problems are expressed in excessive withdrawal, depression, unhappiness, and anxiety. Both types of problems may be found in classrooms.

Achenbach, Howell, Quay, and Conners's (1991) national survey provided a comprehensive analysis of parents' views of problems and competencies of children ages 4–16. This survey was based on parents' reports of a mental health sample of 2,600 children and a matched sample of 2,600 nonreferred (i.e., typically developing) children. Parents rated their children on the ACQ Behavior Checklist (Achenbach, Conners, & Quay, 1983), which includes 216 items measuring both externalizing and internalizing problems. The clinic-referred children received higher (more problematic) scores on 211 items, and large differences were found on items measuring such behaviors as concentration, disobedience, sadness or depression, and cooperativeness. Boys had higher scores on attention problems, delinquent behavior, aggressive behavior, and other externalizing problems, whereas girls scored higher on somatic complaints, anxiety/depression, and other internalizing problems. The findings from this survey provide a comprehensive picture of children's behavior problems as seen by parents and included information about gender, age, ethnic, and socioeconomic conditions. These findings are consistent with earlier surveys by Achenbach and Edelbrock (1981) and Weisz et al. (1987), which also documented the nature and frequency of behavior problems as reported by parents.

Teachers' Views of Behavior Problems

What do teachers view as problem behaviors? Considerable evidence documents consistent views among teachers about problems. Frequently identified problems in three large studies are illustrative (see Table 7.1).

Fergusson and Horwood's (1987) findings were based on teachers' ratings of a sample of 1,103 New Zealand 6- and 7-year-olds. Teachers completed two widely used problem behavior questionnaires developed by Rutter, Tizard, and Whitmore (1970) and Conners (1969). Gagnon, Vitaro, and Tremblay (1992) gathered teachers' ratings of approximately 2,000 Canadian 6- and 7-year-old school children using a French version of the Preschool Behavior Questionnaire (Behar & Stringfield, 1974). This questionnaire is used appropriately with children in preschool through grade two. As part of a large international study, Weisz, Chaiyasit, Weiss, Eastman, and Jackson (1995) included American teachers' ratings of children ages 5–11 on the 118-item Teacher Report Form of the Child Behavior Problems Checklist Form (Achenbach & Edelbrock, 1981). The high frequency prob-

Table 7.1. Researchers' findings of teachers' views of children's problem behaviors

Fergusson and Horwood[a] (1987)	Gagnon, Vitaro, & Tremblay (1992)[b]	Weisz, Chaiyasit, Weiss, Eastman, & Jackson (1995)[c]
Restless, overactive	Restless	Talks too much
Destroys belongings	Blames others	Talks out of turn
Fights frequently	Fights	Hurt when criticized
Bullies	Does not share	Disturbs peers
Irritable	Lies	Easily distracted
Disobedient	Irritable	Messy work
Lies	Bullies	Demands attention
Steals	Inconsiderate	Argues a lot
Squirmy		Fails to finish things
Fidgety		Self-conscious/easily embarrassed
		Misdeed with no guilt
		Disrupts class

[a] New Zealand sample
[b] Canadian sample
[c] American sample

lem behaviors for American children in Weisz' study are included in Table 7.1. Despite the fact that the studies were conducted in different countries and with children of different ages, teachers participating in the study identified common behaviors such as restlessness, overactivity, talking too much, irritablility, bullying, fighting, arguing, and other externalizing problems. Not surprisingly, externalizing problems involving acting out and aggressive, disruptive behaviors were high on the list of problems for teachers, findings confirmed by Forness, Kavale, and Walker (1999) in their recent review. This is not to suggest that internalizing problems such as excessive shyness, poor self-esteem, and anxiety are unrecognized or unimportant, but it does suggest that externalizing behaviors have a greater impact on classrooms, thus they are more commonly recognized as problematic by teachers.

The Relationship Between Temperament and Behavior Problems

Considerable evidence documents the nature and frequency of children's problem behaviors, but relatively little attention is paid to describing the settings in which the child behaves. Yet, from an interactionist perspective it seems clear that except for a relatively small number of organically based problem conditions such as an autism spectrum disorder or Tourette syndrome, extreme conduct disorders, and oppositional behavior, many behavior and adjustment problems occur because they are products or outcomes of incompatible, inappropriate, or negative interactions between the personal characteristics of the child and home and/or school environments. That is where temperament becomes important.

What do we know about the relationship between children's temperament and behavior and adjustment problems? The temperament dimensions described by Thomas and Chess (1977) and other researchers allow normal variations among people and should not be considered problems per se. Particular temperament characteristics, however, may predispose a child to behavior and adjustment problems even if they fall in a normal range when they present challenges to teachers or are a poor fit with teachers' expectations and classroom demands.

Ms. Martinez is an intense young woman in her second year of teaching first grade. She enjoys the children and interacts with them a great deal. She prefers students who, like herself, are quick to respond, eager to try new things, and outgoing and friendly. She has real difficulty working with Carrie, who seems tentative and cries easily. Ms. Martinez often finds herself impatient with Carrie and is unsure whether to push her to become more involved or to leave her alone. Neither finds their relationship positive.

One of the first efforts to relate temperament and behavior problems was by Thomas, Chess, and Birch (1968) as part of the New York Longitudinal Study. Based on parent reports, five major temperament constellations were identified as being related to problems: 1) negative mood combined with irregularity, nonadaptability, and tendencies for withdrawal; 2) excessive persistence; 3) withdrawal and mild negative reactions to new situations combined with slowness to adapt; 4) extreme distractibility; and 5) very high or low activity level. Although these descriptors were gathered a number of years ago, the temperament characteristics are still relevant when considering the nature of children's interactions with others in their environments. The early work of Thomas and colleagues led to the descriptions of "difficult," "easy," and "slow-to-warm-up" children, and stimulated further interest in temperament as a part of the goodness-of-fit notion.

Teglasi and MacMahon (1990) surveyed parents of children 8–12 years of age to determine what behaviors were sources of friction and irritation within the family. Statistical analyses identified five categories of behaviors seen by parents as problematic: proneness to anger and emotional upsets, joylessness/apathy, low self-direction, self-reproach, and oppositional/aggressive behavior. Children's temperaments were then examined relative to the five types of problems.

Temperament dimensions were significantly related to all five categories of behavior. Especially strong associations were found between temperament and problems relating to externalizing problems, specifically proneness to anger/emotional outbursts and aggressive/oppositional behavior. These behaviors are seen in children who respond excessively and intensely when they don't get their way or when they are asked to do something they don't want to do. Children with externalizing acting-out problems may become physically abusive with peers over minor disagreements.

> Jerry is a large and rather clumsy 7-year-old who is quick to anger and quick to behave aggressively and impulsively when he doesn't get his way. On the playground, he often uses his size to push or shove smaller boys when they disagree with him, and his reaction to minor disagreements is excessive. His classmates don't like him and are often intimidated by him.

Further support for associations between behavior problem and temperament is found in the research of Wertlieb, Weigel, Springer, and Feldstein (1987), who, using the Thomas and Chess nine-dimension model of temperament, identified relationships between temperament, stress, "hassles" with parents, and behavior problems in 6- to 9-year-

Table 7.2. Researchers' findings of temperament characteristics associated with behavior problems

Researchers	Behavior problems
Thomas, Chess, & Birch (1968)	Negative mood, withdrawing in new situations, low adaptability, distractible, excessive persistence, extreme activity (high or low)
Wertlieb, Weigel, Springer, & Feldstein (1987)	Negative mood, withdrawing, low adaptability, low persistence, distractible, unpredictable
Teglasi & MacMahon (1990)	Negative mood, low adaptability, low persistence, nonapproaching, high activity
Prior, Sanson, Smart, & Oberklaid (1999)	High active and reactive, low persistence, low approach, low social

old children. Findings confirmed significant relationships between parents' views of children's temperament and behavior problems on eight of the nine temperament dimensions, with associations between temperament and externalizing (aggressive, acting out) problems generally higher than those for internalizing (fearful, depressed) problems. This is not surprising as externalizing problems are apt to disrupt both home and school routines, whereas internalizing problems may be as serious but less intrusive. Findings from different research groups are summarized in Table 7.2.

Findings from longitudinal research are especially interesting as they are based on information collected about the same children at different ages and thus provide some insights about the development of problems. As part of the Dunedin Longitudinal Study, Caspi, Henry, McGee, Moffitt, and Silva (1995) and Caspi and Silva (1995) assessed relationships between the temperament and behavior problems of more than 800 children ages 3–15. As shown in Chapter 2, these researchers had identified three major temperament clusters when the children were age 3: lack of control, approach, and sluggishness. Behavior problems were determined based on ratings by both teachers and parents when the children were ages 9 and 11 and by parents at ages 13 and 15. Temperament in the preschool years was correlated with behavior problems when the children were older, the associations over time being stronger for boys than for girls. The temperament factor of lack of control was especially important in externalizing problems, while negative approach was associated only with internalizing problems.

The Dunedin Study findings are consistent with results from the Australian Temperament Project's assessments of 11- and 12-year-old children's temperaments and their behavior and adjustment problems. Problem children were described as having more difficult temperaments, specifically as being more active and reactive, less persistent, and less approaching and sociable compared to non-problem peers. Many had histories of difficult temperament in toddlerhood, perhaps ". . . predisposing them to the development of negative inter-personal interactions" (Prior, Sanson, Smart, & Oberklaid, 1999, p. 576). The Australian study provides further support for the notion of "difficult" temperament as a contributor to behavior and adjustment problems, but those researchers emphasized that difficultness in infancy was associated with later aggression only if the child was raised in a stressed environment.

The work of Guerin, Gottfried, and Thomas provides a final example. These researchers identified associations between early temperament and later behavior problems. Their study was based on temperament ratings by parents taken when the children were 1 and 1½ years old. Parents' reports of behavior problems were gathered when children were 3 years old and again annually until they reached the age of 12 years, and teachers rated the children from ages 6 to 12 years. Four aspects of temperament in infancy were assessed: difficultness, unsociability, resistance to control, and unadaptability. Guerin et al. found difficultness in infancy to be correlated "significantly and pervasively" with reports of later behavior problems as perceived by both parents and teachers (1997, p. 78). Like others, Guerin et al. cautioned that their findings did not imply that all infants with difficult temperaments will develop behavior problems when older. Rather, the researchers suggested that difficult temperament may be associated with an increase in risk due to "poorness of fit," an interpretation consistent with Thomas and Chess's earlier thinking.

Findings in these studies document relationships between individual differences in children's temperament and behavior and adjustment problems. Although there are some differences in the findings from the different research groups, there is striking agreement across studies. The particularly high agreement regarding characteristics of "difficult" temperament is noteworthy.

TEMPERAMENT AND BEHAVIOR PROBLEMS IN SCHOOL

A point worth re-emphasizing is that not all children with particular, even extreme, temperaments develop problems in school. Temperaments that lead to problems in one classroom may be compatible with the demands in another. The exuberant child who is valued by one teacher because of his enthusiasm and responsiveness may be seen as out of control and intrusive by a teacher who emphasizes order and quiet. This suggests that a broader and more refined view of classroom conditions and interactions is important in order to understand behavior problems in school (Keogh, 1998). These include teachers' views of what is acceptable behavior.

It is reasonable that teachers view children's behavior in the context of classroom routines, and that conforming to rules and "good citizenship" is valued. Teglasi and MacMahon (1990) found that teachers thought of citizenship in terms of how well children work and play with peers, their respect for property and for others, and their responsibility for personal behavior. Good work habits included following directions, completing homework, and listening well. Teachers' ratings of students' classroom behaviors were found to be significantly related to children's temperaments, specifically to predictability and persistence. Their ratings of children on citizenship and work habits were correlated with behavior problems having to do with low self-direction and oppositional/aggressive behavior.

These findings are consistent with those of Guerin, Gott-fried, Oliver, and Thomas, who also reported significant associations between teachers' views of children's temperament and how well they functioned in the classroom. Indeed, in their study, temperament was the "almost exclusive predictor" (1994, p. 219) of classroom behavior. Not surprisingly, teachers were especially sensitive to behaviors such as "how hard does he or she work." The behaviors valued by teachers in both studies are reminiscent of the characteristics of teachable students discussed in Chapter 6.

A reasonable generalization is that individual differences in students' temperaments contribute to their behavior and personal/social adjustment in school. The findings of temperament characteristics making up the "difficult" constellation appear particularly salient in relation to externalizing problems, but temperament is also related to problems of an internalizing nature. As discussed earlier in Chapter 2, Kagan and his colleagues (1989) found that about 10%–15% of the children in their study samples were consistently subdued and wary when facing a novel or unfamiliar situation or challenge. Henderson and Fox (1998) suggested that inhibited temperament may affect children's academic and social competence, as well as their perceptions of their social skills, leading to further withdrawal from interpersonal experiences. Indeed, it might be argued that inhibited children are especially vulnerable in class-

> Mrs. Johanson stresses academics in her eighth-grade classroom and sets extremely high standards. She works especially well with students like Ryan, who sits quietly and diligently attends to the worksheets she hands out. Mr. Lewis, an animated and humorous history teacher, finds Ryan perplexing, however. Mr. Lewis responds well to Kara, who participates often in the lively Socratic discussions he likes to hold with the class. Although Ryan and Kara are both bright, capable students, Ryan feels pressured to perform in Mr. Lewis's class, whereas Kara feels stifled in Mrs. Johanson's class.

room environments and to experiences at school. Compared with more active, assertive children, they are apt to receive less attention from teachers, to have fewer satisfactory social relationships, and to have a limited range of experiences. In addition, they are less likely to be seen as needing special help. Thus, shy and inhibited children also deserve attention.

How Does Temperament Contribute to Behavior and Adjustment Problems?

Particular behaviors and particular temperaments may lead to stress and conflict in homes and in the classroom. But is there a difference between children with extreme or negative temperaments and children with behavior problems? Temperament may contribute to behavior problems, but behavior problems come in many forms and are not necessarily temperament based. Carey suggested that "temperament is a matter of style; behavioral maladjustment means substantial disturbance of social relationships, autonomy, or task performance. A volatile temper is behavioral style; social alienation due to temper is behavioral maladjustment" (1989, p. 132).

This important distinction deserves special consideration when teachers are faced with behaviors that are problems in their classrooms. Certainly, particular temperaments may predispose a child to behave in particular ways, but temperament alone does not explain problems. An important question has to do with the relationship of temperament predispositions and actual problems. Several explanations are plausible.

First, it is possible that temperament and behavior problems are expressions of the same underlying condition but that temperament is evident earlier in the child's development. That is, difficult temperament or extreme shyness evident early on may be the first indication of a behavior disorder that will emerge more clearly as the child grows older. In this interpretation, extreme temperament and behavior problems are considered to be one and the same. Certainly, there is some overlap in the content of both, especially in the constellation of temperament characteristics describing "difficult" children (e.g., distractible, intense, active, and low in persistence). As others have emphasized, however, it is important to remember that not all children with "difficult" or inhibited temperaments develop behavior problems, nor are all children with "easy" temperaments free from problems. Furthermore, individual differences in temperament are recognizable in infancy, and behavior problems appear later in a child's life. Thus, a reasonable inference is that temperament and behavior problems are at least partially independent.

A second plausible explanation is that behavior problems may develop when children's temperament or behavioral styles are reinforced and become integrated or incorporated into generalized maladaptive coping strategies (Carey, 1998). Carey suggested that a child may develop a generalized reliance on individual characteristics, for example, extreme inhibition or extreme activity, as a way of responding to stress, a coping style that is apparent across situations and over time. A child may come to consistently withdraw or act out in order to avoid demanding school tasks or unpleasant social encounters.

Consistent reliance on a maladaptive coping style over time may have broad and often negative effects. This can be seen in Caspi and Silva's (1995) "cumulative continuity effect" in which early stylistic characteristics cumulatively lead to subsequent and often negative consequences. The notion of a cumulative effect of child characteristics and environmental conditions is well illustrated in the monumental work of Werner and Smith (2001),

Peter, a fifth-grader, is usually behind in his academic work and finds most assignments boring and difficult. He has particular trouble when assignments are long. He is low in persistence and is easily distracted. His response to challenges is to play the class clown, disrupting others with silly comments and behavior. As a consequence, he spends many hours in time-out and in occasional trips to the principal's office. These disciplinary measures cut down on his opportunities for instruction but are effective in getting him out of uncomfortable situations.

who, for four decades, have followed a large group of individuals born on the Hawaiian island of Kauai. Their findings clearly document the cumulative contribution of individual biological factors such as temperament to the interactions and transaction with environmental conditions including home and school experiences.

A third explanation for the relationship between temperament and behavior problems is an interactive one. This is based in the bi-directional or reciprocal effects model discussed earlier in Chapter 3 and is fundamental in the notion of goodness or badness of fit. In Chapter 6, it was shown that teachers have remarkably consistent views of the characteristics of "teachable children." Many of those attributes were temperament dimensions. As shown in Table 7.1, teachers have a consistent view of what behaviors are problems. For the most part, problem behaviors are those that are discrepant with teachers' expectations, and that are mismatches between children's behavior and the rules and requirements of the classroom.

Many teachers are frustrated by highly active, impulsive, and intense students, for example, because they may present major impediments to teaching, taking time and attention away from instructional content. Slow-to-adapt and inhibited children also present both instructional and management problems in classrooms, especially classrooms with high demands and limited time. Those children are frequently out of sync with the teacher and with others in the class. Children who are characteristically slow to adapt may also resist new materials and different instructional techniques. They may be seen as unmotivated, uninterested, or even lazy.

From an interactional perspective, how individual differences in temperament interact with environmental demands leads to behavior adjustment or behavior problems. In this case, temperament is a contributor to but not a direct cause of behavior problems. This view means getting away from thinking of problems as "in the child" and rather of thinking of problems in terms of the "child in context."

SUMMARY

Clinical and educational literatures contain descriptions of the impact of individual differences in children's temperament on their behavior and adjustment, and specific temperamental characteristics have been linked to behavior problems. Several explanations for these links have been proposed. The most plausible is that temperament and behavior problems are best understood within an interactional model that takes into account characteristics of the child, the teacher, and the classroom. Agreement also exists that certain constellations of temperament, particularly those describing "difficultness," may predispose a child to problems, but that temperament and behavior problems are not one and the same.

CHAPTER 8

Temperament and Children with Disabilities

Individual differences in children's temperaments contribute to the range and nature of their experiences and to the kinds of interactions children have with others. In this chapter, the particularly powerful way in which temperament influences children with disabilities is discussed. All children profit from individual attention, but children with disabilities may place particular demands on adults that affect the nature of interpersonal relationships. Children with disabilities often require extra and sometimes specialized responses and help from teachers. A teacher may need to work closely with a child with a learning disability to develop assessments in line with curriculum and standards. A child with a physical disability may need a special keyboard to write assignments, assistance getting down stairs to go to recess, or help in getting on the bus for a field trip. Another child with cognitive limitations may require a specialized instructional program and a great deal of direction and monitoring in the classroom. A child with a severe hearing impairment may need individual attention when assignments are made, or a child may require a specialized regimen for taking medication.

Teachers' responses to such special needs relate in part to children's personal characteristics, including temperament. Some temperament patterns are likely to lead to positive, supportive relationships, while others may lead to stressful interactions. Like children without disabilities, children with disabilities bring a range of individual differences to the classroom and to their lives at home. The point is well illustrated by parents' descriptions gathered from interviews of their young adults with developmental delays who participated in Project Reach, a longitudinal study of children with developmental delays and their families (Bernheimer & Keogh, 2001). When asked to talk about their child, parents responded with such descriptions as, "She is very easy"; "Everything he does is slow. He takes his time"; "She is irritable, fussy. She is just not pleasant to be around"; "He's a good kid, a happy, energetic child"; or "She's friendly and pleasant and agreeable." These descriptions tapped behavioral styles, not cognitive abilities, and as in most interpersonal interactions, suggested that individuals with special needs who have positive temperaments are perceived as easier to interact with than are those with negative, difficult styles.

Karla, 8 years old, has a mild hearing impairment. She is shy and withdrawn and doesn't often raise her hand or react enthusiastically to assignments. Mrs. Zeller, her first-grade teacher, knows that Karla sometimes fails to write down the homework assignments and doesn't like working in teams. She struggles to find ways to get Karla more involved and on task. Mrs. Zeller hates to admit it, but sometimes days go by when she doesn't call on Karla or ask her to participate in group activities.

From this perspective, temperament characteristics may serve as powerful protective or risk factors in the lives of children with disabilities. Positive, easy temperaments increase the likelihood of healthy interpersonal interactions with family members, teachers, and friends, and reinforce feelings of personal and social competence. Alternatively, a difficult temperament may add to the problems that confront a child with disabilities, increasing his or her isolation and disrupting interpersonal relationships both at home and at school. Two children may have similar cognitive or physical limitations, yet one may be positive in mood, adaptable, and approaching and sociable and the other may be intense, withdrawing, and negative in mood. Teachers may work more effectively with the former than the latter, and the experience of school will likely differ for the children themselves.

WHAT DO WE KNOW ABOUT TEMPERAMENT AND CHILDREN WITH DISABILITIES?

Many researchers have described the impact of disabling conditions on children's experiences in families and in schools, and in general the findings are that children with disabilities are at increased risk for psychosocial maladjustment. Important to note however, is that considerable variation exists among individuals and their families in outcomes; some children lead happy and productive lives, whereas others have many problems in adjustment and social relationships. Similarly, families differ in how they adjust to a child with disabilities; some families respond adaptively and positively to children's conditions, whereas others find these conditions disruptive to family life. Why there are such differences in outcomes is not entirely clear, but the degree of functional independence of the children and the number of daily challenges seem to make for smooth- or rough-going experiences at home and at school.

Wallander and Varni's review of research on the impact of children's chronic physical disorders on family adjustment is informative. Their review indicated that approximately 10%–20% of children in Western developed countries have chronic conditions that affect their daily functioning, often leading to incidents of hospitalization, which make them vulnerable for maladaptive outcomes. Chronic conditions are viewed as those that are persistent, require continual responsiveness and readjustment, and may interfere with daily activities thus resulting in "ongoing chronic strain" (1998, p. 31).

How children and adults react to ongoing disabling conditions affects the quality of life for both. Wallander and Varni (1998) proposed that risk factors for adjustment include the nature of the ongoing conditions and their functional impact on the activities of daily life (ADLs). Factors include

- Characteristics of the child, such as competence, motivation, and temperament
- Social-ecological conditions such as family adaptation, social support, and resources
- Stress-producing factors such as how the disability is perceived and the nature of coping strategies

Wallander and Varni's review of research underscores that there are multiple contributors to outcomes for children with ongoing physical disorders and their families.

Considerable evidence from a number of different research groups suggests that temperament may be one of the contributing influences, though compared with the number of studies of temperament in children without disabilities, temperament in children with disabilities has received relatively little attention. Several studies suggesting that temperament plays a role in the experiences of children with disabilities are relevant, however. In the Australian Temperament Project, Prior, Glazner, Sanson, and Debelle (1988) found that mothers of children with hearing impairments rated their children as having difficult temperaments compared with a matched group of hearing children. Bailey and colleagues (1998) found that trained research staff rated children with fragile X syndrome (a condition often associated with mental retardation) and a subgroup of those with autism as slower to adapt, less persistent, and more withdrawing than a comparison group of children without disabilities. Varni, Rubenfeld, Talbot, and Setoguchi (1989) found that emotionality was associated with poor adjustment in children with chronic physical disorders.

As in any group, a range of individual temperament differences exists among children with disabilities. Some children with physical or cognitive disabilities are easy, some are slow to warm up, and others are difficult. The important question is, of course, how these differences in temperament contribute to the nature of the experiences of children with disabilities and to their interactions with the adults and peers around them. Carey and McDevitt (1995) suggested that differences in temperament might influence children's responses to hospitalization and to how they respond to illness and medical care. Some adapt easily to restrictive regimens, others are overintense and prone to anger. Garrison, Biggs, and Williams (1990) found that the temperament characteristics of high activity, low rhythmicity, and low attention span were related to problems in compliance and monitoring of a medically determined regimen for children with diabetes, for example. Temperament influences in children's responses to medical treatments may be especially salient as many children with disabilities often face ongoing and stressful medical interventions. Carey and McDevitt speculated that "children involved in extensive and arduous therapeutic procedures for their ongoing medical condition or disability would demonstrate an increase in adherence and success proportional to their endowment with the characteristics of adaptability and persistence" (1995, p. 106).

Individual children with disabilities also respond differently to the school environment. Children's temperaments also evoke different responses from educators who provide special services for them (e.g., teachers and staff involved in medical procedures for children with physical limitations and needs). The tempera-

Lenny has severe physical limitations because he has cerebral palsy (CP). His speech is often difficult to understand and both his large and fine motor skills are very poor. As a result he is restricted in term of playground activities and has difficulty doing school assignments that require writing. He is also one of the most popular children in his class. His teacher describes him as "good-natured and a great kid." He adapts easily to changes in assignments and is diligent in completing his school work, even though his motor skills require a great deal of effort.

ments of both child and adult play roles here, affecting the nature of the individuals' interactions. An inhibited and unresponsive child who needs daily medication and a busy school nurse who has limited time may not work well together, for example. Similarly, interactions between a difficult and aggressive child with severe hearing loss and a special education reading teacher who is new to the field may be tense and unsatisfying for both. The experiences of these children with adults are likely to be markedly different from the child with disabilities who has an easy temperament.

Two groups of children with disabilities are particularly relevant to this discussion of temperament in the classroom. These groups include children identified as having a learning disability and those with cognitive or intellectual delays.

Temperament and Children with Learning Disabilities

Children identified as having a learning disability (LD) make up almost one half of all students receiving special educational services and approximately 5% of the school population in general (U.S. Department of Education, 1998). A number of researchers have described children with LD as low in task orientation, persistence, and adaptability (Bender, 1985, 1987; Cardell & Parmar, 1988; Keogh, 1983, 1994; Martin, 1989). The work of Pullis (1985, 1989), who studied children identified with LD, is particularly interesting because he related children's temperamental characteristics to teachers' decisions in the classroom. He found that both inclusive and resource room teachers rated elementary school children with LD as low in task orientation and adaptability and high in reactivity compared with peers without LD. He also documented that task orientation significantly influenced teachers' decisions about behavior management and increased their need to monitor children's behavior in classroom situations.

Although there is agreement that as a group, children with specific learning disabilities are low in task orientation, it is important to emphasize that the term *learning disabilities* captures a wide range of specific problems and that, within any group of students identified as having LD, there will be differences in temperament. Thus, when making clinical or educational decisions for individual children with LD, generalizations about temperament must be made cautiously, taking into account the unique characteristics of each child.

Temperament in Children with Developmental Delays

Children with developmental delays (DD) compose a second and relatively large group of children receiving special education services. The broad term DD subsumes a number of specific conditions that have in common impairments in intellectual skills relative to like-age peers. In some cases, the causes of the conditions are known, as with, for example, Down syndrome, which is genetically based. In others, the etiologies are uncertain. Because one of the defining characteristics of DD is cognitive delay, children with DD often require special instructional programs and make up a significant proportion of students in special education. The role of temperament in these children's school experiences, thus, deserves consideration.

As part of the NYLS, Chess and Korn (1970) found that the ratings of children identified as having mental retardation were similar to peers without mental retardation on the nine Thomas and Chess (1977) dimensions of temperament but that there was considerable variability among individual children in both groups on the dimensions. For example, activity ratings ranged from high to moderate, intensity ratings from mild to variable, and mood ratings from positive to variable. University of California, Los Angeles (UCLA), researchers confirmed that there were many differences in temperament in children with cognitive delays of unknown etiology and that individual differences on the dimensions of distractibility and persistence were significantly associated with behavior problems for children with delays (Keogh, Bernheimer, Haney, & Daley, 1989). Wilson (1999) found that children with developmental delays were more intrusive and aggressive than their peers without developmental delays and that they also were less able to regulate their emotions in response to social situations.

Because children with Down syndrome can be identified early in life, they have been one of the most-studied groups of children with disabilities. Interestingly, evidence of the validity of the stereotype that children with Down syndrome are good-natured, placid, approaching, and in temperament terms, easy, is mixed. Some findings are consistent with this picture (Gunn & Berry, 1985), but other researchers have found little support for the stereotype. Indeed, Bridges and Cicchettti (1982) reported that the infants with Down syndrome in their study were low in persistence and approach and had low thresholds of stimulation. Ratekin (1990) found that the percentages of preschool children considered easy or difficult were similar for comparison groups of children with and without Down syndrome and were comparable to the percentages reported by Thomas and Chess in the NYLS sample. In that study, 40% of the children in the NYLS were considered easy and only 10% were seen as difficult. Ratekin also found that some differences in how children were perceived depended on whether quantitative ratings of specific temperament dimensions (e.g., activity level, persistence, mood) or global impressions (e.g., easy, difficult, slow-to-warm-up) were used. In general, global impressions yielded more favorable pictures than did ratings of specific dimensions.

Researchers at the Hospital for Sick Children in Toronto, Canada, have carried out a series of studies focused on temperament in young children with developmental delays, including children with Down syndrome, children with delays of unknown etiology, and children with confirmed neurological problems (Goldberg & Marcovitch, 1989; Marcovitch, Goldberg, MacGregor, & Lojkasek, 1986). In this work, differences among diagnostic groups on ratings of temperament dimensions were documented. The children in the group with neurological problems had the highest ratings on distractibility and approach, and the Down syndrome group had the highest ratings on activity. Based on global impressions, children with Down syndrome were perceived as easier than were children in the other two disability groups. Like Ratekin (1990), the Canadian researchers found somewhat different impressions of children with Down syndrome depending on whether temperament was assessed by global impressions or by ratings of specific dimensions.

It is important to remember that there is no single temperament profile that describes all children with developmental delays. Some are easy, some are difficult, some are adaptable, some are inflexible, some are persistent, and others are distractible. Students with disabilities bring a wide array of temperaments to the classroom, and these individual differences can lead to satisfactory or unsatisfactory experiences in school.

Temperament and Attention-Deficit/Hyperactivity Disorder

Although attention-deficit/hyperactivity disorder (ADHD) is not considered a disability per se, attention deficits and hyperactivity are frequently proposed as the basis for children's poor adjustment and low achievement in school, and the diagnosis of ADHD is widely accepted by both medical and educational professionals. ADHD is also controversial. Specific diagnostic criteria vary and have changed over time, but almost all diagnoses require evidence of early onset (before age 7), persistence over time, disruption of daily activities, and presence before other disorders such as depression. Experts differ in their views about the causes of ADHD, the specificity of underlying neurological conditions, the contributions of the environment, and how ADHD should be treated. Swanson (1992) asserted that a number of conditions (e.g., anxiety, depression) may lead to ADHD-like symptoms. That is, the ADHD behavioral characteristics may be, in part at least, a reaction to extreme anxiety or depression.

Despite some inconsistencies in diagnostic criteria, experts usually agree that ADHD is a real condition that affects the lives of children and their teachers in many ways. Many of the characteristics associated with it are similar to descriptors of temperament. Some, but not all, children with ADHD are highly active and impulsive; they have problems sitting still, sustaining attention, and controlling their behavior and they are distractible. Because some of the characteristics are similar to those described as temperament characteristics, the two may be confused at times. Just because someone has certain temperament traits that are associated with ADHD it doesn't mean that he or she has ADHD. Compared with temperament-related behaviors, the behavior of children with ADHD is excessive in degree and goes beyond the characteristics of children with difficult temperaments. The problem, of course, is to determine what defines *excessive*. Though the *Diagnostic and Statistical Manual of Mental Disorders–Fourth Edition–Text Revision* does not specify the exact criteria for "excessive" behaviors, it does describe school-age children with ADHD in the following way: "They have difficulty remaining seated, get up frequently, and squirm in, or hang on to the edge of, their seat. They fidget with objects, tap their hands, and shake their feet or legs excessively" (American Psychiatric Association, 2000, p. 86).

Carey and McDevitt noted that it is often unclear how excessive activity level must be in order to be considered hyperactivity or ". . . at what point normal inattentiveness turns into a pathological attention deficit" (1995, p. 150). Several points are relevant, however. ADHD behavior is not only extreme, but as noted earlier, it is also ongoing and consistent. The behaviors are apparent in the classroom, on the playground, in the cafeteria, in organized games, or in informal activities with friends. Furthermore, the behaviors are not dramatically modified when the situation or the instructional tasks are changed.

In contrast, many temperament-based behaviors are most apparent in particular situations and respond to modifications in the organization of the classroom and the setting. Although temperament patterns may predispose a child to problems, as discussed in Chapter 7, stylistic differences are not the same as problems. Carey pointed out that "a volatile temper is a behavioral style: social alienation due to temper is behavioral maladjustment" (1989, p. 132). Clearly, individual differences in temperament affect children's adjustment and achievement in school. Individual characteristics of temperament are usually best thought of as "normal variations" that are not in themselves problems.

In this regard, it is important to emphasize that differences between temperament and ADHD need to be recognized so that the popular diagnosis of ADHD is not overused or misused, as the diagnosis has implications for treatment, including the use of medication. Similar to characteristics of temperament in children with disabilities, there will be individual differences in temperament among children with ADHD, and not all children with particular temperament profiles will have ADHD. The point underscores the need to consider children's behavior and misbehavior within a goodness-of-fit model.

Brian was extremely active as an infant and preschooler and continues to be so, creating many disruptions in family and school routines. He is now in the fourth grade, and his teacher, Mrs. Rodriguez, a quiet woman, finds him difficult to manage. He speaks in a loud voice and frequently gets up and wanders around the room. Yet he is a bright boy and a good reader. He has problems on the playground where he is very rough. Mrs. Rodriguez will consider her own temperament and instructional techniques and use observational data from these different contexts when communicating with Brian's parents and with any school professionals who might be involved in assessing Brian's behavior.

Considering temperament may be useful for teachers and school psychologists when they are considering referring a child for evaluation of ADHD. A first step in understanding problem behavior in the classroom means considering the context of the classroom and the instructional program. Temperament-related problems are often closely tied to specific situations and events, whereas problems related to ADHD are more generalized and evident over time. Identifying individual differences in temperament and classroom interactions within a goodness-of-fit model can help determine which temperament-based problems are situationally specific and which are more serious and pervasive conditions. Also, working closely with parents and other teachers and professionals in the school system, such as those who serve on a student's individualized education program (IEP) team, can help educators get a full picture of a student's behavior and temperament across contexts. Of course, this is a good strategy for children with any type of disability, not just those who may have ADHD.

HOW DOES TEMPERAMENT INFLUENCE THE BEHAVIOR AND ADJUSTMENT OF CHILDREN WITH DISABILITIES?

Findings suggest that there may be some temperamental characteristics associated with particular disabilities but that the temperament of children with disabilities differs widely. There is no single temperament stereotype or profile of children with disabilities.

Some children with disabilities are task oriented and adaptable; others are distractible, intense, and lack persistence. Some are approaching and interactive; others are withdrawn and shy. Children also differ from each other in mood, in the ways they interact with others in their classrooms and on the playground, and in how they approach social situations. An interactionist perspective holds that these differences in behavioral styles will elicit different responses from teachers and peers. These differences also affect the ways children with disabilities respond to new tasks or assignments and their willingness and ability to modulate and direct their activity and to monitor their behavior.

Children may be limited by the nature of their disabilities, and temperament may add to these limitations, restricting opportunities for new experiences and interactions with peers. Think of a child with a physical disability who is withdrawing and shy or a child with developmental delays who is low in adaptability and low in activity. In contrast, temperament may serve to broaden the experiences and opportunities for children with disabilities. Children with disabilities who are positive in mood, who are approaching and adaptable, and who experience life fully and enthusiastically enjoy a wide range of experiences and opportunities and are likely to have positive relationships with others. Indeed, temperaments of children with disabilities may have a particularly powerful impact on interactions with others, as the additional demands of a child's disability on parents and teachers may be mitigated or intensified by the child's behavioral style and temperament.

Keogh and Burstein (1988) observed preschool children with developmental delays and their peers without disabilities in three school situations: in a large group, in a small group, and on the playground. On measures of task orientation and personal/social flexibility, teachers rated the children without disabilities higher than they rated the children with delays. On measures of reactivity—usually seen as a negative attribute— teachers rated children without disabilities lower than those with disabilities.

The most important finding in this study was that the patterns of teacher–child interactions differed for the two groups. Overall, teachers interacted more with children without disabilities who had positive temperaments than they did with those children with negative temperaments. The pattern was different in the group of children with DD; teachers interacted more with children with DD with negative temperaments than those with positive temperaments. These findings make sense when considered with the discussion of teachers' perceptions and decisions in Chapter 6.

Still another influence of temperament in children with disabilities has to do with children's sense of their own attributes— their own abilities to deal with demands. Strelau (2001) suggested that children differ in their abilities to deal with stress and to moderate how they deal with the intensity of their environments. A child with a low sensory threshold may react strongly to the hubbub in the school cafeteria at lunchtime. That level of stimulation may be especially difficult for a distractible child with attention problems or for the child with cognitive processing delays. Children with physical disabilities can cope in games on the playground differently depending on their degrees of persistence and adaptability.

Focusing on children identified as having mental retardation, psychiatrist Stella Chess wrote that "certain patterns of temperament appeared to intensify the stresses to which the retarded child is especially subject in his interaction with the environment" (1974, p. 263). On the positive side, she noted that "temperament . . . may influence the child's ability to make use of environmental efforts to help him toward optimal functioning" (p. 264).

Because children with disabilities often require special attention and time, the contribution of temperament may be a particularly important influence on their relationships with teachers. How teachers perceive individual differences in temperaments among children with disabilities will affect the frequency of their interactions, and perhaps more importantly, the affective nature of the interactions. In some cases teacher–child interactions will be relaxed and warm; in other cases they may be only efficient. The admonition for teachers to understand themselves and their attitudes is especially relevant when working with children with disabilities.

SUMMARY

Studies have shown that individual differences in temperament are found in groups of children with disabilities, that the range is similar to that found in peers without disabilities, and that there are some differences in temperament according to the method used in collecting temperament information. Individual differences in temperament may serve as risk or protective influences for children with disabilities, affecting their relationships with adults and peers and the range of their experiences. Easy temperaments may mitigate the affects of extra demands associated with disabling conditions whereas difficult temperaments may increase stress for children and adults alike. There is no single pattern of temperament associated with particular disabilities.

CHAPTER 9

How Is Temperament Assessed?

At the turn of the 21st century, educators are being held accountable for student learning and achievement as never before. Assessing students is a major activity in schools, and there are many different approaches and methods. Teachers use daily assignments and teacher-made tests to determine how much students are learning and what instructional modifications are needed. School personnel assess students yearly with standardized achievement tests tapping specific subject-matter areas and basic skills. School psychologists use individual tests to assess children's abilities and personalities. Assessing students is important in documenting how effectively students learn and, by implication, how effectively teachers teach.

Teaching and learning are the lifeblood of schools, so it makes sense that many assessments in school are focused on describing children's intellectual aptitudes, their language proficiencies, and their achievement in subject matter areas. Assessment is particularly critical when students have achievement problems. Interestingly, teachers usually don't ask why students behave as they do when they are doing well.

Educators are especially concerned when things aren't going well for a student, such as when a student is having academic or adjustment problems. The goal is to find out what is the matter, why, and what to do about it. When children are having academic problems, educators quite understandably focus on students' cognitive abilities using standardized IQ measures and language skills. These provide important information, but tap a relatively narrow range of children's attributes, and do not get at *how* children perform.

This is where temperament comes into play. Although not as extensive as methods for assessing cognitive and achievement domains, a number of approaches for assessing temperament have proved useful and are available to teachers and school psychologists.

THREE APPROACHES TO ASSESSING TEMPERAMENT

The three most common approaches to assessing temperament are interviews, observations, and rating scales or questionnaires. With the exception of some laboratory measures that involve physiological technologies, such as an electroencephalogram (EEG), these approaches rely on someone making a judgment about a child's temperament based on the child's behavior or more specifically, on behavioral style—the "how" of behavior. Adults, mainly parents, teachers, or others who know the child well, usually complete the temperament assessments. This, of course, raises questions about objectivity.

Parents' views of their children's temperament may be selective, may reflect parental expectations and bias, and may change over time. The same is true for teachers. As discussed in previous chapters, teachers' expectations for a child's behavior in school, their own values, and their past experiences with a child or even with a child's siblings or parents may influence their views of a child. Teachers also have many experiences with children over time, which allow them to recognize consistencies in individuals' behaviors and temperaments. For the most part, teachers rely on unstructured, even casual ways to describe children's temperaments, but teachers may enhance their sensitivity to individual differences in children by using established temperament assessments. Each of the three types of assessments is described briefly.

Interviews

Interviews provide opportunities for teachers to gather detailed pictures of children from people who know them well, usually their parents. Indeed, discussion of children's strengths and weaknesses is an important part of parent–teacher conferences. Many interviews are informal, taking place when a parent picks up a child after school or volunteers in the classroom or library. Other interviews are formal, for example, when a parent comes for the regularly scheduled semester conference or to talk about a particular problem.

Whether informal or structured, interviews provide opportunities to learn about a child's temperament in a relatively short time and to document stabilities and changes in behavioral styles over time and in different situations. Teglasi (1998) suggested that interviews are especially useful because information documenting continuities and discontinuities in the child's temperament can be identified, and information about the child's life experiences out of school can be gathered.

Mr. Hollingsworth, a seventh-grade social studies teacher, finds Ray a constant irritant. Ray is a high achiever who is very verbal and is not shy about challenging him. In Mr. Hollingsworth's view, Ray is being purposely obstructive. Not surprisingly the two are often at odds. Mr. Hollingsworth met with Ray's parents and, after explaining the Thomas and Chess dimensions, asked them to describe their son in these terms. With the additional insights gleaned from Ray's parents, Mr. Hollingsworth realized that he and Ray are both intense and quick to react. As a follow-up, Mr. Hollingsworth began ongoing discussions with Ray that helped them understand that their temperaments, while sometimes causing them to be antagonists, could also help them to become allies.

Discussions with parents help teachers determine whether a child's behavior is specific to school or whether the same stylistic characteristics are also evident at home. Parents can also provide background information about children's earlier school experiences and insights about how they deal with temperament-related difficulties or problem behaviors at home. Interviews with parents also provide a way for teachers to gather information that might be relevant to children's behavior at school. Are there stresses at home that account for a child's negative mood? Are there physical conditions that might affect a child's energy and enthusiasm?

School psychologists who work with children who have behavior or adjustment problems will find interviews with both parents and teachers a good source of information. Interviews with teachers are especially important because teachers are primary sources of information about children's day-to-day behaviors in the classroom. Teachers' views, as well as those of parents, provide psychologists with a more complete picture of children than can be determined from tests and allow insights into the effects of classrooms and peers on children's behaviors. Interviews may also be useful when used in conjunction with rating scales because interviews provide opportunities for elaborating the findings from structured questionnaires.

Observation in Laboratory and Classroom Environments

We are all observers of other people's behaviors, although in everyday life few of us use systematic ways of describing behavior. Nonetheless, we often hear such comments as "That kid can never sit still"; "She is always in a good mood"; "He is constantly on the go"; or "Nothing seems to bother him." Those generalizations about someone else are based in large part on observations over time and situations, observations that have built up a picture of another person's behavioral style. When applied in school, observations can be a useful way of documenting a student's behavioral style while at the same time pinpointing possible trouble spots.

Laboratory Studies   Observation carried out in laboratory environments is an important part of temperament research. Laboratory studies may have limited direct application to how the individual behaves in the "real world" of classrooms because methods often address only a limited array of behaviors. Studies have contributed significantly to understanding the bases of temperament and have documented characteristics of temperament that are relevant to clinical and educational applications, however.

Controlled studies in laboratories have proven especially useful for researchers because they provide information focused on specific behaviors in specific situations. They also allow the use of high tech methods to document neurological and physiological aspects of temperament. As discussed in Chapter 4, Fox, Henderson, Rubin, Calkins, and Schmidt (2001) used electrophysiological methods to describe patterns of brain activity in inhibited and exuberant children. Rothbart, Derryberry, and Posner (1994) identified brain systems underlying the development of reactivity and regulation. Kagan, Reznick, and Gibbons (1989) also used physiological measures to study children's tendencies to be shy and inhibited.

Naturalistic Observations   Observations of individuals in natural environments such as classrooms provide a way of documenting temperament in the everyday world. Naturalistic observations may be highly specific or global, formal or informal, or based on samples of time or samples of events, but the goal is to provide a picture of an individual's behavior in context. There are a number of different approaches to observations in the classroom. Some require an independent observer who can document the behaviors of teachers and students. Some observational systems are highly structured and detailed so that all children in a classroom might be observed at different but specified times (time samples)—for example, every 2 minutes or when in particular situations such as math instruction or individual seat work (event samples). Other observational approaches may focus on a given child for longer periods of time, at different times of day, or in different situations. See Atkins, Pelham, and Licht (1988); Evertson and Green (1986); and Greenwood (1996) for discussion and examples of observational systems.

Mrs. Graham enlisted the help of a "floating" teacher's aide to observe her fourth-grade classroom during reading and social studies. Over 3 days, the aide recorded the number of interruptions by students (e.g., talking out of turn, off-task behavior) and Mrs. Graham's responses to these behaviors. The aide documented that three students in the class were the most disruptive, although most of students were restless during the last 15 minutes of group instruction. The observer also noted inconsistencies in Mrs. Graham's responses: Sometimes she ignored students who were misbehaving and sometimes she publicly reprimanded them. Based on these data, Mrs. Graham adjusted her lectures and assignments and made sure that she responded quickly and directly, but non-punitively at the first signs of problems.

Systems also differ in the level of detail targeted. For example, the observer may focus on the number of times a particular child looks about the room and is off task or the number of times the child interrupts another student. Another observer may be interested in how much teacher time is spent in talking to the whole class and how much time is spent working with individual students, or the frequency of praise and reprimands. Greenwood's (1996) ecobehavioral system is an observational approach that takes into account components of students' behavior, teachers' behavior, and the nature of the setting, thus allowing the specification of functional relationships and interactions among them. Greenwood has found that his observational system, the Code for Instructional Structure and Student Academic Response (CISSASR), and the versions adapted for mainstream settings and preschool, provide lenses for examining instructional outcomes and pinpointing where change is needed.

Observation is not always formal and systematic, however. Teachers make informal observations of students every day in the classroom. These observations form a snapshot of a child that becomes the basis for teachers' decisions about how to work with that child. Sometimes the pictures are accurate, other times they are not. A teacher may be particularly sensitive to certain behaviors, with the result that some behaviors may be overlooked and others overemphasized. Thus, the picture may not be a good representation of a child. This may be particularly true when subtle aspects of temperament are considered.

Assessing the Five "Ws" The use of focused observations can sharpen teachers' views of temperament-related behaviors of children in their classrooms without interfering with classroom routines, however. Tharp and Gallimore (1988) have provided a helpful way to think about classroom environments and children's behavior. They propose the notion of "activity setting," suggesting that classroom activities can be described by five "Ws": Who, What, When, Where, and Why. *Who,* of course, refers to who is there—two children, a small group, a child and teacher, or the whole class? *What* describes the things that are being done, including the "scripts" that determine how things are done. For example, children may be asked to read in a small group at a time determined by the teacher. The script requires the children to take turns reading and to be quiet while each child reads aloud. *When* refers to the timing and schedule of the activity: for example, when in the day reading, arithmetic, or geography is taught; for how long; and at what pace. *Where* describes students' location in the classroom; this may vary for particular instructional or management purposes. *Why* involves both meaning and motivation. A lesson may be interesting and important from the teacher's perspective but the same lesson may be irrelevant from a student's perspective. In that case, there is little reason for the student to engage in learning.

Children's reactions and behaviors may vary because their behavioral styles interact with the five "Ws." For example, some highly distractible and low-persistence children may have difficulty in group environments but work better when with only one other child or with a particular child. A small-group project on map making may be of real interest for the teacher and a few children but not motivating for others, leading to off-task behavior—especially for high-activity, distractible children. For an impulsive child who has trouble persisting, waiting for long periods to get help from the teacher may trigger the child to behave inappropriately. Using activity settings as a framework is a way to systematize observations across classroom situations. Sensitivity to the five "Ws" provides teachers a way to focus observations of children within the context of the instructional program and the classroom as a whole.

Because temperament interacts with the circumstances and the demands of the classroom, it makes good sense that observations must cover different situations and different times. Children may behave very differently at school than they do at home. Similarly, their behavior may vary at school, depending on whether it is just an ordinary day or whether a special event is scheduled, such as a parent's visit to the classroom or a special occasion such as a field trip or the fall harvest parade and party day. Students may behave differently when in a small group discussion or when looking up material in the library. An active, talkative child may be uncharacteristically quiet on the first day of school or when faced with a test he or she is not prepared for. A slow-to-warm-up child may

Ms. Mendoza, an outgoing and popular kindergarten teacher, was having difficulty working with Karen, who was exceptionally quiet and who did not participate in the noisy give and take of classroom activities. Unsure whether Karen's behavior was a sign of something serious or just a personality type very different than her own, Mrs. Mendoza decided to observe her closely over several days. She made notes throughout the day as Karen moved from solo deskwork to group-work and play situations. Ms. Mendoza gave her notes to the school psychologist, who had Mrs. Mendoza and Karen's parents complete a few selected assessments in order to identify how to help Karen adjust to the school program.

be outgoing and interactive only after several weeks in the class-room or when with a small group of friends.

Whatever the observational plan, an important question is this: How consistent is the child's behavior across situations? Is the child fidgety and overactive in free play as well as in formal instructional periods? Is the child consistently reticent and shy when first arriving at school or when faced with changes in classroom routines? Observing children's behaviors in different environments and at different times of the day allows a teacher to build a reliable picture of a child's temperament and to pin-point areas of possible problems and areas of adaptation. Thus, observations must cover different contexts and different times, and both the behavior and the environment must be taken into account.

Some Cautions   Like other information-gathering tech-niques, observational data gathering may be affected by the skills and sensitivity of the observer. Furthermore, formal sys-tems for collecting data may not be relevant or specific to the purpose of the observation, or they may be so broad that they do not address particular behaviors or conditions. Observations fo-cused on aggressive behavior miss documenting problem be-haviors associated with excessive shyness, and observations lim-ited to student behavior cannot take into account the impact of teacher behavior. A time sampling system in which every child in the room is observed in a set order for 2 minutes may miss an important event involving another child. Similarly, event-based observations focused on a particular classroom activity such as math instruction do not capture what happens in the reading period.

Nonetheless, both naturalistic and laboratory observations are useful ways to assess children's temperaments and behavior. Thoughtful observation of children in the classroom can provide teachers with insights about individual differences in children's behavioral styles that are clues to how to organize and manage classrooms and schedules that maximize positive interactions.

Good observation over time is one of a teacher's most powerful tools.

Rating Scales/Questionnaires

The most common method of gathering information about temperament is with questionnaires and rating scales. This is, in part, because of the ease of getting information and because it is relatively efficient and inexpensive in terms of time when compared with observations and interviews. Before describing some of the most widely used questionnaires and scales, it is important to note some of the limitations of this method. This is not to question the usefulness of questionnaires in assessing children's temperament, but rather to remind raters of necessary cautions in interpreting rating-scale data.

Martin identified a number of sources of potential errors in ratings. Some have to do with the raters themselves. As Martin noted, ". . . a rating is a measure of the frame of reference of the rater as well as a measure of the behavior of the child" (1988, p. 7). Different people bring different frames of reference to the rating task, and thus see children's behaviors from different perspectives. Two teachers may rate the temperament of the same child somewhat differently—one seeing a child's high activity as interfering and intrusive—another seeing the same behavior as a sign of vigor and enthusiasm. A second potential error in rating comes from the effects of possible influences of the setting. Children's behaviors may change or be modified in part because of the situation in which they find themselves. A child's persistence may be different when he is working alone at his desk or in a group lesson, when he is doing something he likes to do or something he finds boring.

Martin also underscored the fact that children's behaviors are not always consistent, even in the same setting. Most teachers have seen children's behavior in the classroom change as the school week continues. Some children come to school on Monday morning eager and "ready to go," but by Friday, they are tired and stressed. Other children find the Monday morning transition from home to school difficult, but their adjustment improves as the week progresses.

Finally, when different assessment instruments are used, there is always the potential for differences in findings. For example, eight or nine temperament dimensions are rated in the Thomas and Chess (1977) questionnaires, while three are identified in the Buss and Plomin (1984) scale. Instruments for assessing temperament differ somewhat in the constructs measured, in the response format used, and in the level of detail of items—all of which may affect findings.

Given these cautions, however, it is important to emphasize the usefulness of questionnaires for assessing temperament. Reviews by Teglasi (1998) and Keogh and Bess (1991) are good sources of information about a range of scales. These authors stress the need to consider measures in terms of the purpose of assessment, breadth or specificity of content, validity and reliability, age appropriateness, potential biasing effects, and psychometric qualities. They also conclude that questionnaires provide a way to gather information that enhances understanding of students' behavior and that can inform instruction. A number of questionnaires and scales are psychometrically sound and have documented utility in assessing children's temperament. Several commonly used questionnaires and scales appropriate for use with pre- and school-age children may be found in Appendix B.

Scales Based on the Thomas and Chess Model of Temperament Scales based on the Thomas and Chess model of temperament include the following:

- Carey scales: Pediatrician William Carey and his colleagues developed many of the most widely used questionnaires within the Thomas and Chess formulation of temperament, including the Carey Temperament Scales (Carey, 2000), which consist of the Revised Infant Temperament Scale (RITQ) (Carey & McDevitt, 1978), the Toddler Temperament

Scale (TTS) (Fullard, McDevitt, & Carey, 1984), the Behavioral Style Questionnaire (BSQ) (McDevitt & Carey, 1978), the Middle Childhood Temperament Scale (MCTQ) (Hegvik, McDevitt, & Carey, 1982), and the Early Infancy Temperament Questionnaire (EITQ) (Medoff-Cooper, Carey, & McDevitt, 1993).

- The Child Temperament Questionnaires (CTQs) for parents or teachers (Thomas & Chess, 1977)
- The Dimensions of Temperament Survey (DOTS) (Lerner, Palermo, Spiro, & Nesselroade, 1982) and the Dimensions of Temperament Survey–Revised (DOTS–R) (Windle & Lerner, 1986)
- The Short Form Teacher Scale (TTQ-S) (Keogh, Pullis, & Cadwell, 1982)

Scales Based on Other Models of Temperament   Assessment instruments have been developed for other formulations of temperament not based on the Thomas and Chess model, as well:

- The Children's Behavior Questionnaire (CBQ) for parents (Rothbart, Ahadi, & Hershey, 1994)
- The Colorado Childhood Temperament Inventory (CCTI) (Rowe & Plomin, 1977)
- The Emotionality, Activity, and Sociability Scale (EAS) (Buss & Plomin, 1984)
- Martin questionnaires: Questionnaires by Martin and his associates are widely used for assessing temperament in school age children. They include the Temperament Assessment Battery for Children (TABC) (Martin, 1988) and the Temperament Assessment Battery for Children–Revised (TABC–R) (Martin & Bridger, 1999).
- The School-Age Temperament Inventory (SATI) (McClowry, 1995) is a parent report inventory directed at four aspects of temperament: task persistence, approach-withdrawal, negative reactivity, and energy. The items cover a range of behav-

ior relevant to both home and school (e.g., "Gets very frustrated"; "Has difficulty completing assignments").

- The Temperament and Atypical Behavior Scale (TABS) (Bagnato, Neisworth, Salvia, & Hunt, 2002)

Informal Assessments

Finally, several clinical approaches to understanding temperament have focused on "difficult," or in Kurcinka's term, "spirited" children. Kurcinka describes spirited children as those who are ". . . more intense, persistent, sensitive, perceptive, and uncomfortable with change than other children" (1998, p. 7). She recommended that parents develop a picture of their spirited child based on temperament attributes similar to those in the Thomas and Chess model. In Kurcinka's model, each attribute is rated, yielding a quantitative score that can be combined to describe a child as "cool," "spunky," or "spirited."

Although they did not create formal questionnaire, Turecki and Tonner (2000) provided descriptions of difficult infants, toddlers, preschoolers, and young children and posed questions that can serve as a framework for parents to use in describing their child. Both Kurcinka and Turecki and Tonner have focused on parents, but their approaches to understanding temperament can reasonably be used by teachers for thinking about temperament in students and in themselves.

FACTORS INFLUENCING FINDINGS

This chapter describes a number of different ways to assess children's temperament. With the exception of some of the neurophysiological techniques, these methods are based on the perceptions or views of another person, usually a parent, teacher, psychologist, or researcher, and thus there may be differences in findings. Similarly, descriptions of children's temperaments may vary in different situations or environments and at different times, making it important to assess children's temperaments in different contexts. It should be noted, too, that the kind of temperament information gathered depends also on the model of temperament followed. Somewhat different temperament profiles result when the assessment is based on different formulations, as for example, the Thomas and Chess (1977) model or the Buss and Plomin (1975) model.

In addition, as pointed out by Goldberg and Marcovitch (1989), several levels of specificity of temperament information can be gathered. At one level, parents or teachers may rate items regarding specific behaviors: "Child's responses are loud"; or "Child can continue at the same activity for an hour" (Thomas & Chess, 1977). Ratings may also target broad temperament dimensions: "He is persistent"; "She is adaptable"; or "She is approaching." Ratings may also be made on global impressions using broad categories or types: "He is easy"; "She lacks control"; "He is sluggish"; or "She is difficult."

Ratekin suggested that global impressions are generalized, abstracted views of a child's temperament and that "because perceptions are based on multiple experiences with a child, it is likely that they are heavily influenced by context and may reflect . . . how problematic each adult finds a child's particular behavioral style" (1990, p. 21). As a result, discrepancies based on different levels of information can occur. Despite these differences a number of methods have acceptable validity and are useful for teachers and school psychologists in assessing children's temperament.

ASSESSING TEACHERS' TEMPERAMENTS

Information about children's temperament is only part of the picture. Common themes throughout this book are that the relationship between adults and children is interactive and that understanding children's experiences in school requires taking into account the context of the classroom, including the temperament of the teacher. Consider first the teacher–child interactions. Think about how an active, fast-moving, and intense teacher can affect the school behavior of an inhibited, shy, and withdrawing child. Think of the nature of the interactions between a reactive, distractible, and impersistent child and a task-oriented teacher. Think also about the likelihood of stressful interactions when both teacher and child are intense and inflexible. Because teachers influence children and children influence teachers, the temperaments of both are important.

Relatively few formal approaches for assessing temperament in adults as compared with those used with children are used, but several examples are described briefly as appropriate for use with adults. As noted in Appendix B, the Adult Temperament Questionnaire (ATQ) (Chess & Thomas, 1995) and the Dimensions of Temperament Survey–Revised (DOTS–R) (Windle & Lerner, 1986) may be used with adults. Kurcinka (1998) suggested that parents become aware of their own temperaments by rating themselves on characteristics of intensity, persistence, sensitivity, perceptiveness, adaptability, energy, first reaction, and mood. For example, intensity ratings might range from 1 (*mild*) to 5 (*intense*), and first reaction ratings from 1 (*jumps right in*) to 5 (*rejects at first*). Turecki and Tonner (2000) did not suggest specifically that parents *assess* their own temperaments, but their recommendations for working with difficult children clearly encourage increasing self-awareness, which is part of the goodness-of-fit concept. The importance of being aware of one's own temperament is equally relevant for teachers. The point is that teachers need to recognize how their own temperaments influence their classroom behavior and their interactions with students.

Closely related, understanding temperament in the classroom means taking other aspects of context into account. Clearly, children differ in how they adjust and respond to the organization of the classroom, the scheduling of instruction, and the daily routines that direct behavior. From this perspective, teachers and classrooms as well as students need to be considered in assessment. Broadening the scope of assessment to include classroom conditions and practices may at first make teachers uneasy and apprehensive. But such information can benefit overworked teachers who must manage the many complexities of a classroom. Teachers' awareness of the context of classrooms and their own temperaments can provide insights that improve the quality of experiences in school for both students and teachers.

SUMMARY

Interviews, observations, and questionnaires are all valid ways to assess temperament. Differences among assessment techniques as well as differences in findings related to rater, situation, and time of assessment are possible, of course. The notion of activity setting can be used as a framework for teachers' observations in the classroom. When thinking about assessing temperament, it is also important that educators be aware of their own temperaments because individual differences in teachers' behavioral styles contribute to how classrooms function and consequently, to how students adjust and achieve.

How Can Temperament Knowledge Be Applied in School?

Teachers and other school professionals work directly with children on a day-to-day basis. They spend months with children who have unique aptitudes and abilities and different educational and personal needs, who bring different experiences to the classroom, and who are different in temperament. Earlier chapters established several basic tenets regarding temperament:

- Real, individual differences can be found in children's temperaments or behavioral styles.
- These differences affect the nature and breadth of children's experiences both within and outside the classroom and contribute to the ways they approach learning tasks.
- Children's relationships with teachers and peers are best understood within an interactionist framework.
- Temperament contributes to the goodness of fit between child and school.

In addition, earlier chapters looked at temperament from a number of perspectives: What is it? Why is it important? How does it contribute to adjustment and achievement? How does it influence interactions with others? How can it be assessed? The important question now is this: How can knowledge of temperament be applied in the classroom?

Knowledge of temperament applications in the classroom is useful to educators in three powerful ways. First, teachers will find thinking about temperament helpful in understanding their attitudes toward and their interactions with students. Second, recognizing individual differences in temperament helps anticipate where stresses and problems are apt to occur. Third, understanding temperament provides direction to classroom management and interventions.

TEMPERAMENT, TEACHERS' ATTITUDES, AND TEACHER–CHILD INTERACTIONS

Given the number of pressures on teachers' time, attention, and energy, it would be reasonable for them to view thinking about temperament as just another demand that adds to their level of stress. In fact, awareness of individual differences in temperaments can have the opposite effect, helping teachers alleviate stress by increasing their understanding of the basis of their attitudes and their interactions with particular children. This in turn can lead to appropriate tailoring of interventions, interactions, and academic programs to respond to students' individual differences.

Educators have numerous interactions with students every day, during and outside of school hours. Some interactions are planned, others occur spontaneously. Some are positive, leading to productive outcomes; others are negative, resulting in unsuccessful and stressful interchanges. These differences reflect, in part, the match between teacher and child. It is instructive, thus, to review briefly the notion of goodness of fit as it is basic to understanding temperament in school.

Goodness of Fit Revisited

A number of aspects of goodness of fit are important in classrooms. What is the nature of the match between children's abilities and interests and the content of the instructional program? Is there a good match between teachers' skills and children's aptitudes and knowledge level? How well do children's behavioral styles match the demands and constraints of the classroom, including teachers' temperaments and expectations? A poor fit between children's temperaments and the daily demands and routines of the classroom often leads both teachers and students to feel frustrated and angry or even incompetent or guilty.

A major theme in this book is that individual differences in children's temperaments contribute to their experiences and to the goodness of fit between the child and the demands of school. Individual differences in children's temperaments are only one part of the notion of goodness of fit, however; the context of the classroom and the characteristics of the teachers also contribute. Like students, classrooms and teachers differ, and both affect the nature of the fit between the child and school. It is possible, even likely, that the nature of the fit between the individual child and school will be different in different classrooms. For example, 7-year-old Donovan may be overstimulated and overwhelmed in a high activity, "free-wheeling" classroom but may get along well in a structured program. Naomi may find the high-activity classroom interesting and involving but may be somewhat bored in slower paced programs. Ms. Omara may work well with exuberant children, while Ms. Kennedy finds them difficult. Differences in children, in classroom contexts, and in teachers thus must all be considered as all contribute to goodness of fit.

Children's behavioral styles and how they affect achievement and adjustment in school have been described in detail in earlier chapters. The importance of classrooms and teachers in the goodness of fit equation also deserve brief discussion.

Goodness of Fit and Characteristics of Classrooms

What do we know about classrooms that affect goodness of fit? What aspects of classrooms should be considered? On the one hand, a number of structural conditions exist over which teachers have no control: the number of students in the room, the time schedule for the school as a whole, the reading program mandated by the school district, or whether classrooms have individual desks or shared tables. On the other hand, teachers determine how classrooms function, the pace of activities, and the rules of behavior. Who sits where? What are the traffic patterns to get to the board, to the teacher's desk, or to the pencil sharpener? How is the make-up of groups determined? How are transitions from one lesson to another or from classroom to play yard organized? How much time is allowed for reading or for arithmetic?

Nicole is a bright but shy, slow-to-warm-up 9-year-old who initially felt uncomfortable when Mr. Chang, the teacher, called on her. Fortunately, Mr. Chang recognized Nicole's behavioral style and initially made a point of calling on her only when he was confident Nicole knew the correct response. He also made sure Nicole was not among the first children called on, thus giving Nicole time to prepare her thoughts. The teacher's tactics worked well, and now Nicole is more comfortable, has gained confidence, and has become a more active participant in classroom activities.

Classrooms differ in organization and requirements, and students differ in how they respond. Children's temperaments as well as their aptitudes and interests interact with the content, scheduling, and pace of instruction; the organization and the use of space; and the teacher's instructional styles. In some cases, these interactions lead to effective and efficient learning. In others, the results are not so positive.

Goodness of Fit and Characteristics of Teachers: "Know Thyself"

Another component of goodness of fit has to do with the temperament of the teacher. Teachers bring their own unique temperaments to the classroom that affect their interactions with students. Thus, teachers need to be aware of their own behavioral styles. Like children, some teachers are quick to respond, active, and intense. Others are reflective, quiet, and slow to warm up. Some are distractible, others are persistent, some are easily irritated, and others are even-tempered and easy. These differences affect their relationships with students and contribute to the overall affective tone of the classroom.

Children's and teachers' temperaments may go well together or may be at odds. A slow-to-warm-up teacher may be especially understanding of a shy and inhibited child, whereas another teacher may be impatient with the child. This does not imply that the best fit necessarily comes when teacher and child have similar temperaments. Consider the potential stresses in the interactions between an active, intense, and reactive teacher working with an excitable child with a similar temperament profile. Sparks can fly and minor disagreements or misunderstandings can easily escalate into confrontations because both teacher and student are apt to act quickly and impulsively. A less impulsive and less intense teacher may work effectively with the same child, tolerating or even valuing the child's behavioral style. In another example, when a teacher who is slow to warm up is paired with a child who is similar in temperament, both may have trouble connecting with each other. The key for teachers is to recognize their personal styles and to be aware of how these individual characteristics influence their relationships with students.

For teachers, "knowing thyself" also means recognizing the expectations they have for students' behavior. Chapter 6 discusses teachers' views of teachable students and what they believe students ought to be like. Many of the characteristics teachers listed as making up a teachable child describe temperament, but not all students in any classroom fit a positive profile. Teachers vary in how they respond to these differences, particularly if the children's temperaments are discrepant from what the teacher views as desirable. It is not so much the particular characteristics as it is how those characteristics are perceived and how they contribute to the fit between child and teacher that matters.

"Knowing thyself" is also closely related to being aware of the range of individual differences that define one's perception of acceptable behavior. Teachers differ in their "zones of tolerance." Some find a wide range of children's behaviors acceptable; others tolerate only a narrow range. Loud, impulsive, talking-out-of-turn behaviors bother some teachers but are ignored by others. Fidgety, out-of-seat behavior draws a reprimand from some teachers but only a mild reminder from others. The breadth of the zone of teacher tolerance affects classroom environments, and determines in part what behaviors and what students are perceived as problems. "Knowing thyself" is an important part of goodness of fit and must be considered when thinking about how temperament affects life in the classroom.

HOW CAN AWARENESS OF TEMPERAMENT HELP EDUCATORS ANTICIPATE PROBLEMS IN THE CLASSROOM?

Understanding temperament helps teachers anticipate problem situations that may arise with students. As discussed earlier, classrooms are complex environments with many demands, and students differ in how they respond to these demands. Some students adjust easily to classroom rules and routines but other do not. We can anticipate stresses when children's behaviors are not consistent with classroom routines and teachers' expectations for their behavior.

Most children adapt quickly to the routines and demands of the classroom, but temperaments of a few children may present problems. Recall that 40% of the children in the New York Longitudinal Study were considered easy, 15% were slow to warm up, and 10% were considered difficult (Thomas & Chess, 1977). Kagan, Reznick, and Gibbons (1989) found only 10%–15% of children in their studies to be truly inhibited, numbers consistent with the exuberant children identified by Fox, Henderson, Rubin, Calkins, and Schmidt (2001). This means that if there are 25 children in a classroom, it is likely that only five or fewer will be considered "difficult" or inhibited. This does not imply that children with extreme temperaments do not present particular challenges. Indeed, teachers may spend excessive and stressful time with those children. It comes as no surprise that in general, teachers prefer and are comfortable with children with easy temperaments because those students adapt well to both instructional and management requirements that make for smooth-running classrooms.

Recognizing how differences in children's temperaments affect their behavior in the classroom and their reactions to classroom routines allows teachers to anticipate problem situations and to take preventive measures, thereby reducing the stress levels for both students and teachers. The five "Ws" (Who, What, When, Where, and Why) described in Chapter 9 provide a useful framework for describing classrooms and help pinpoint problem situations and times. Knowing that classroom routines are apt to be disrupted at particular times in the day, when certain children are working together, or when new instructional materials are being introduced can help teachers plan ahead to avoid problems. This information serves two purposes that are closely linked: It makes it possible to anticipate problems

Mrs. Collins has worked hard to establish a stable daily routine in her second-grade classroom. Each morning she goes over the schedule for the day and draws the children's attention to possible changes or special events that might affect the regular routine. As the day progresses, she often reminds the students that the time to move on to another activity (e.g., from reading to math) is coming up. Her efforts have been especially helpful for the children who find transitions difficult and who are bothered by newness and change.

and it focuses interventions. The old adage, "Forewarned is forearmed," is appropriately applied to classrooms.

HOW CAN TEMPERAMENT BE USED TO PLAN INTERVENTIONS?

As noted previously, anticipation can lead to positive preventive strategies. Recognizing how individual differences in students' and teachers' temperaments affect the nature of life in school also provides directions for responding to particular behaviors. It is interesting that despite the increasing awareness of temperament, relatively little attention has been directed at applying temperament in schools, and there are few formal temperament-based programs directed at classrooms and teachers. This is in contrast to programs for parents in which a number of intervention/treatment approaches have been developed.

Temperament-Based Programs for Parents

Psychiatrists, clinical psychologists, and pediatricians use temperament when working with individual children and families (see Bates, 1989; Carey, 1989, 1997; Carey & McDevitt, 1995). Temperament-based programs and publications that are focused on parent training and on ways parents can deal with temperamentally different children are also available. Several of these are described in Appendix C and provide ideas for applying temperament knowledge in schools.

APPROACHES TO TEMPERAMENT-BASED INTERVENTIONS IN SCHOOLS

Temperament-based programs for parents contain a number of relevant points for teachers interested in temperament-based interventions in schools. The first and most obvious is to recognize and appreciate individual differences in children's temperaments. On the surface this seems easy, but it really requires a different way of thinking about children and their behavior. Not surprisingly, teachers tend to think about children in intellectual or motivational terms. Comments such as "She is not very bright," or "He doesn't work hard," reinforce the idea that problems are based in the children. Sensitivity to temperament allows teachers to think about children differently, to reframe their ideas about the reasons for particular behaviors, and to consider problems in a different context. The overall effect is to lower the level of negative affect and frustration teachers often feel when there are problems.

Reframing Perceptions and Attributions

Viewing behavior in temperament terms allows teachers to reframe or recast their ideas about the reasons for students' behaviors. This is especially true in regard to problem behaviors. In many cases, teachers have ideas about the reasons for the problems, but the reasons are often general and imprecise (e.g., "problems at home," "a mean kid," " bad company," "hates school," "won't try," "not very bright"). Because the attributions about the causes of the problems are imprecise, strategies about what to do are frequently ineffective, the problematic behavior continues, and the teacher becomes more frustrated. That is where reframing or recasting the problem in temperament terms comes into play.

Viewing children's behaviors as pertaining to individual differences in temperament can change and broaden adults' views about the meaning of behaviors and the reasons why children behave as they do. This is not to suggest that all problems are temperament related. Certainly there are children who have severe and ongoing problems that require specialized and intense professional help. Many problems in the classroom may be explained as mismatches between classroom demands and children' behavioral styles, however. Consider how problems may arise when a highly active, reactive, and distractible child is in a crowded classroom or is faced with long stretches of time with little to do. Similarly, a shy and withdrawing child may have problems when in a program with many demands for quick adaptations to different activities. Such problems probably are not due to serious "in-child" conditions. Rather, they are evidence of a poor match to classroom demands, a mismatch that has consequences for teachers' responses and children's performance.

An example is the inhibited child who has trouble adapting and who is upset at any change in the routine of the classroom. If the child's behavior is seen as a deliberate, attention-getting technique or as lack of motivation, the child is apt to be ignored or reprimanded. If the behavior is seen as part of the temperament constellation of "slow to warm up," the teacher can consider ways to prepare students for changes (e.g., letting them know how much time remains to finish an assignment or signaling that transitions are coming up). Reframing or recasting children's behaviors into a temperament framework reduces the level of affect or emotion. It also provides directions for intervening in positive ways as it pinpoints needed and often obvious changes such as the following:

- Allow more time to complete assignments.
- Cut down on unnecessary interruptions and distractions.
- Provide opportunities for some quiet time.
- Provide opportunities for physical activities and fun.

Broadening the Basis of Assessment

Another intervention step is to broaden the range of assessment information. Because schools are focused on teaching and learning, it makes sense that many assessments in school describe children's intellectual aptitudes, language proficiency, and achievements in subject-matter areas. Yet children's performance in school is clearly influenced by other personal characteristics, including temperament. If we take seriously the idea that there are multiple contributors to children's successes and problems in school, it is clear that teachers need to consider a range of potential influences, and students' behavioral styles are important possibilities.

Viewing behavior from an interactionist perspective also means gathering information about the context in which students and teachers work. This implies that school psychologists and other specialists need to carry out at least part of their assessments in classrooms because that is where the action takes place. In addition to information about the organizations and routines of the classroom, important information includes teachers' views of desired and acceptable behavior, their views of what students "ought to be like," and their comfort levels or "tolerance zones" in dealing with individual differences among students. All of these interact with students' characteristics to affect goodness of fit; thus, all are important in planning interventions.

By describing classrooms, school psychologists and other specialists can help teachers see how the content and organization of the program affect students' behavior and performance and they can help identify problem situations and times. Assessment information can also document how teachers' attention may be inconsistent, leading to some children being overlooked or ignored. Assessment, whether formal or informal, is useful when it enhances teachers' awareness of individual differences because those insights provide direction to prevention and intervention.

Planning and Implementing Interventions

Intervention means taking some action to bring about change. Important questions include "What should be changed?" and "How can change be accomplished?" A first step in intervention is to identify the problem and when and where it occurs. Rather than dealing with globally defined problems such as "attention deficit" or "acting out," the focus needs to be on specific behaviors that are troublesome and the situations in which they occur. It also helps teachers to determine which behaviors are the most problematic and truly unacceptable and which are merely annoying. Describing behaviors in this way leads to a more objective assessment of what is happening, where, and when. It also allows targeted efforts to bring about change and, thus, focuses intervention efforts. Table 10.1 contains suggestions for teachers

Table 10.1. General strategies for anticipating and intervening with students with various temperament types

Know thyself

Be aware of your own temperament and behavioral style.

Recognize your expectations for students' behavior and achievement.

Ask yourself why you find some students easy, difficult, or slow-to-warm-up.

Identify which student behaviors annoy/upset or please you.

Understand your "zone of tolerance" or comfort level for particular behaviors.

Analyze the reasons you think are the basis for problem behaviors.

Anticipate problems

Be aware of differences in students' temperaments and behavioral styles.

Consider the fit between your temperament and students' temperaments.

Use observation to identify consistent trouble spots and times.

Analyze when problems occur by time of day and by day of week.

Review the organization of space in the classroom relative to individual difference in behavioral styles.

Review the organization of the instructional program relative to individual differences in behavioral styles.

Intervene when necessary

Establish a consistent daily routine for classroom activities.

Make your expectations for students' behavior clear and concise.

Use observation to identify who, when, where, and under what circumstances problems occur.

Use observation to document what works well.

Decide what behaviors are truly unacceptable and focus on those.

Determine which problems are temperament-related due to a poor fit with classroom demands.

Modify classroom routines as needed to respond to trouble spots.

Minimize unnecessary transitions, interruptions, and distractions.

Consider individual differences in temperament in how you organize space, traffic patterns, and seating arrangements.

Consider the content and timing of the instructional program relative to individual differences in students' temperaments—too little or too much time.

Help students understand their own behavioral styles and how they interact with classroom and instructional requirements.

Intervene before problems escalate.

to consider when planning interventions that take into account individual differences in temperament.

Intervening in Temperament-Related Problems

Two ways to think about intervening with temperament-related problems in the classroom are to focus on the situation or to focus on the child. This chapter has already discussed how an understanding of temperament helps educators anticipate situations that have a good chance of leading to troublesome behaviors, including transitions, traffic patterns that disrupt other children, and standing in line for long periods of time. These situations are particularly problematic for children with "difficult" temperaments but can be trouble spots for many students, and unless educators respond to these situations, they can lead to conflicts.

Ms. Coles has learned that Ronnie becomes easily overexcited when something unusual occurs in the classroom. On a recent trip to the zoo, she made sure he sat near her on the school bus and she calmed him down at the first signs of overexcitement by giving him a verbal reminder and a supportive wink. Knowing his temperament helped her prepare him for stressful situations and events and reduced the likelihood of problem behavior.

Intervening with Active and Intense or Slow-to-Adapt Children

The situational approach to intervention is to consider how conditions can be changed to reduce the probability of problems. Teachers can think through the daily routines of the classroom and organize them so that long periods of idle time between activities are minimized, thus decreasing the likelihood that the highly active, intense, and reactive child will begin to act up.

Organizing transitions to avoid long lines to go to lunch or recess reduces the probability of disruptive behavior, especially

Table 10.2. Strategies for working with difficult students

Know thyself

Be specific about what behaviors you expect.

Recognize what behaviors are problems for you. Be specific.

Ask yourself why this child "bugs" you.

Think of the fit or lack of fit between your temperament and the child's temperament.

Anticipate problems and intervene when necessary

Consider possible reasons for the child's misbehavior.

Avoid generalized calls for good behavior.

Identify where, when, and under what circumstances problem behaviors occur.

Consider possible sources of distraction (e.g., child seated next to pencil sharpener, to the door to the hallway, to the gerbils' cage).

Keep instructions direct and concise; don't overwhelm or confuse students with long and complex instructions.

Don't offer options or choices if there really aren't any.

Minimize and organize transitions to avoid confusion and long periods of time spent standing in lines.

Reduce idle and long waiting times.

Provide opportunities for motor activity.

Offer the child suggestions of ways to replace unacceptable behaviors with acceptable ones.

Avoid confrontations and power struggles by anticipating problems and intervening early.

for difficult children. All children in the classroom do not need to line up at the same time. Children can be excused by row or table. The order of this task can be rotated so that each group gets to be first on a regular schedule. Children can also take turns being the "line leader" or calling groups to come forward and get in line. The route to the pencil sharpener or the teacher's desk does not have to be intrusive to other students. Seating arrangements can be changed to minimize conflict. These are organizational and management issues that have powerful effects on how classrooms run, especially the impact on the behavior of highly active and intense children. Some strategies for working with difficult children are found in Table 10.2.

Thoughtful management based on sensitivity to children's temperaments often leads to improved classroom environments

Table 10.3. Strategies for working with shy and slow-to-warm-up students

Know thyself

Ask yourself how you interpret inhibited and slow-to-warm-up behavior styles.

Consider whether these behaviors are problems for you.

Analyze how much of your time and attention goes to these children compared with their classmates. Is your time equitably spent?

Think of the fit or lack of fit between your temperament and the child's temperament.

Anticipate problems and intervene when necessary

Develop a daily routine that provides consistency and familiarity to classroom activities.

Analyze the scheduling of instructional tasks—too much or too little time?

Help students get started on assignments. Make starting instructions brief, clear, and orderly—be available to help early in the assignment.

Signal students regarding how much time remains to complete assignments.

Alert students to upcoming changes in classroom daily routines. Talk about future novel events well in advance. Minimize surprises.

Don't require immediate involvement in group activities. Let students become involved at their own speed.

Choose students' work partners or "buddies" carefully. Don't overwhelm a shy child with an active, quick-responding, and intense partner.

Don't push. Encourage!

for all students. Slow-to-adapt children or those who are highly task-oriented and persistent are apt to be upset by the many transitions and interruptions in a school day. They benefit from reminders by the teacher that they need to move to the next assignment or that a change in the routine is upcoming. Children with low thresholds of response are often overstimulated and overwhelmed in crowded and high-activity classrooms because they are especially sensitive to the many sights, sounds, colors, and activities that are characteristic of rich classroom environments. They need space, a quiet spot, and "down time," and may profit from opportunities to work alone or with only one or two other students. Having to answer questions in front of the whole class may trouble very shy children because the very "publicness" of reciting out loud makes many children anxious. Table 10.3 contains suggestions for working with shy and slow-to-warm-up children.

Helping Children Self-Direct Their Own Behavior

Another way to think about interventions is to consider how children can be helped to modulate and direct their own behavior. Increasing children's awareness of their own temperaments is a step toward helping them manage themselves. This does not mean educators should provide children with excuses for misbehavior. Rather, it is a way to help children anticipate when and in what circumstances they are apt to have problems and to increase their ability to regulate their responses.

HELPING STUDENTS TO KNOW THEMSELVES

Teachers are critical in helping students understand their own temperaments and the implications of these individual characteristics for behavior in school. Like other areas of learning, it takes students time, support, and lots of discussion with teachers in order to understand their own temperaments and to recognize how to anticipate and modulate their behavior. One strategy is for teachers to describe and discuss their own behavioral styles with students, to reinforce the idea that individuals, including teachers, differ in temperament and that these personal differences are to be valued as they are part of what makes each person unique.

Kevin is an excitable, impulsive child who often overreacts. Mrs. Bradley helps him learn to monitor his own behavior, to recognize when he is getting overstimulated, when his voice is becoming too loud, and when his behavior "nears the edge." Once recognized, he can intervene for himself, for example, by withdrawing briefly from classroom activities or even by relying on the proverbial "count to 10 and take a deep breath" strategy.

Teachers can help students become aware of their behavioral styles and how those styles fit or don't fit with classroom demands. As with teachers' views, reframing the behavior into temperament terms allows children to understand some of the reasons for their behavior in a nonpejorative and positive way. Students can be helped to recognize what classroom situations are stressful for them, and to anticipate where and when they may have problems. They can also be helped to learn ways to monitor or modify their own behavior to prevent problems from developing. Slow-to-warm-up students can learn strategies for organizing and beginning assignments. Active and intense-responding children can become sensitive to signs of overstimulation and the need to pull back and modulate their behavior. Shy and reticent children can become more confident and interactive when they recognize social situations that fit their styles or, conversely, situations that make them anxious and uneasy.

Through ongoing discussions about temperament, teachers and students can learn mutually supportive ways to work with each other. At the same time, teachers can learn what cues are helpful to individual students. They can become sensitive about *how* to help students, *when* to help, and *when* to stand back. Such discussions between teachers and students about temperament need to be low key, relaxed, and confidential. It is important that the temperaments of both teachers and students are part of these conversations, and that the emphasis is on how being aware of the temperaments of both can lead to more positive interactions. Reframing can help both students and teachers to know themselves and each other.

Finally, interventions must be considered in relation to individual children and their temperaments. McClowry (1998) emphasized that a specific intervention may not be optimal for all children, challenging the "one size fits all" notion. Indeed, a positive intervention for one student may be ineffective or even have negative consequences for another. McClowry illustrated his point with time-out, a widely used intervention strategy for helping children "cool down" and reduce disruptive behavior. This intervention is often effective, but McClowry noted that time-out might have other consequences. It may reward students with low persistence as it allows them to get out of working on difficult assignments. Time out that takes a student out of the classroom may also reinforce acting up behavior because it provides students with a way of avoiding schoolwork and classroom demands.

Chapter 7 discussed thinking about the development of behavior problems through a temperament lens, suggesting that particular behaviors such as extreme withdrawal or excessive activity may become generalized coping styles when children are faced with stressful situations. Specific interventions, thus, need to be considered in light of both short- and long-term consequences for children with different temperaments. Appropriate and effective interventions must take into account a range of individual differences among children. Temperament is surely not the only issue of importance, but thinking of temperament can provide insights and ideas about improving the goodness of fit between children and school. Sensitivity to individual differences in temperament also increases the probability of positive experiences for both students and teachers. These goals ultimately foster student achievement.

SUMMARY

How can temperament be applied in the classroom? This chapter poses approaches based on three questions: 1) How does temperament contribute to teachers' interactions with students? 2) How does awareness of individual differences in temperament allow teachers to anticipate where problems and conflicts may occur? and 3) How does understanding temperament foster classroom management and interventions? Specific topics include revisiting goodness of fit, "knowing thyself," reframing perceptions and attributions, broadening the basis of assessment, and planning interventions. The importance of an interactionist framework for understanding students and classrooms is emphasized.

We have learned a great deal about temperament since Thomas and Chess's early work, work that has had such a powerful effect on the way development is understood. Many of the ideas in this book are based on their work. Consider the following quotes:

> The school makes a number of new demands on the child, separately and in combination. These include the mastery of increasingly complex cognitive tasks, and the simultaneous requirements to adapt to a new geographic setting, to strange adults in unfamiliar roles, and to a host of new rules and regulations. (Thomas & Chess, 1977, p. 93)

> The degree to which parents, teachers, pediatricians, and others handle a youngster in a manner appropriate to his temperamental characteristics can significantly influence the course of this psychological development. The oft-repeated motto, 'Treat your child as an individual,' achieves substance to the extent that the individuality of a child is truly recognized and respected. (Thomas, Chess, & Birch, 1969, p. 202)

We have all benefited from Thomas and Chess's thinking, and they deserve our thanks. Given the importance of their contributions, it is appropriate to conclude this book about temperament and schooling by reflecting on their words.

Bibliography

REFERENCES

Achenbach, T.M., Conners, C.K., & Quay, H.C. (1983). *ACQ Behavior Checklist*. Burlington: University of Vermont, Department of Psychiatry.

Achenbach, T.M., & Edelbrock, C. (1981). Behavioral problems and competencies reported by parents of normal and disturbed children aged four to sixteen. *Monographs of the Society for Research in Child Development, 46,* Serial No. 188, 1–81.

Achenbach, T.M., Howell, C.T., Quay, H.C., & Conners, C.K. (1991). National survey of problems and competencies among four-to-sixteen-year-olds. Parents' reports for normative and clinical samples. *Monographs of the Society for Research in Child Development, 56*(3), Serial No. 225, 121–130.

American Association of University Women. (1992). *How schools shortchange girls.* Washington, DC: American Association of University Women Educational Foundation.

American Psychiatric Association. (2000). *Diagnostic and statistical manual of mental disorders* (4th ed., Text rev.). Washington, DC: Author.

Atkins, M., Pelham, W.E., & Licht, M.H. (1988). The development and validation of objective classroom measures for conduct and attention deficit disorders. *Advances in Behavioral Assessment of Children and Families, 4,* 3–4.

Bagnato, S.J., Neisworth, J.T, Salvia, J.J., & Hunt, F.M. (1999). *Temperament and Atypical Behavior Scales (TABS): Early childhood indicators of developmental dysfunction.* Baltimore: Paul H. Brookes Publishing Co.

Bailey, D.B., Mesibov, G.B., Hatton, D.D., Clark, R.D., Roberts, J.E., & Mayhew, L. (1998). Autistic behavior in young boys with Fragile X syndrome. *Journal of Autism and Developmental Disorders, 28,* 499–508.

Bates, J.E. (1989). Applications of temperament concepts. In G.A. Kohnstamm, J.E. Bates, & M.K. Rothbart (Eds.), *Temperament in childhood* (pp. 321–355). Chichester, England: John Wiley & Sons, Ltd.

Bates, J.E. (1989). Concepts and measures of temperament. In G.A. Kohnstamm, J.E. Bates, & M.K. Rothbart (Eds.), *Temperament in childhood* (pp. 1–26). Chichester, England: John Wiley & Sons, Ltd.

Bates, J.E., Maslin, C.A., & Frankel, K.A. (1985). Attachment security, mother–child interaction, and temperament as predictors of behavior problem ratings at three years. In I. Bretherton & E. Waters (Eds.), Growing points in attachment theory and research. *Monographs of the Society for Research in Child Development, 50*(1–2), Serial No. 209, pp. 176–193.

Behar, L.B., & Stringfield, S. (1974). A behavior rating scale for the pre-school child. *Developmental Psychology, 10*, 601–610.

Bell, R.Q. (1968). A reinterpretation of the direction of effects in studies of socialization. *Pychological Review, 75*, 81–95.

Bender, W.N. (1985). Differences between LD and non-LD children in temperament and behavior. *Learning Disability Quarterly, 8*, 11–18.

Bender, W.N. (1987). Behavioral indicators of temperament and personality in the inactive learner. *Journal of Learning Disabilities, 20*, 301–305.

Bernheimer, L.P., & Keogh, B.K. (2001). *Project REACH interviews: Technical report.* Los Angeles: University of California.

Bridges, F.A., & Cicchetti, D. (1982). Mothers' ratings of the temperament characteristics of Down syndrome infants. *Developmental Psychology, 18*, 238–244.

Buss, A.H., & Plomin, R. (1975). *A temperament theory of personality.* New York: John Wiley & Sons.

Buss, A.H., & Plomin, R. (1984). Revised temperament survey. In *Temperament: Early developing personality traits.* Mahwah, NJ: Lawrence Erlbaum Associates.

Cardell, C.D., & Parmar, R.S. (1988). Teacher perceptions of temperament characteristics of children classified as learning disabled. *Journal of Learning Disabilities, 21*, 497–502.

Carey, W.B. (1985). Temperament and increased weight gain in infants. *Developmental and Behavioral Pediatrics, 6*, 128–136.

Carey, W.B. (1989). Clinical use of temperament data in pediatrics. In W.B. Carey & S.C. McDevitt (Eds.), *Clinical and educational applications of temperament research* (pp. 137–140). Amsterdam/Lisse: Swets & Zeitlinger.

Carey, W.B. (1989). Practical applications in pediatrics. In G.A. Kohnstamm, J.E. Bates, & M.K. Rothbart (Eds.), *Temperament in childhood* (pp. 405–420). Chichester, England: John Wiley & Sons, Ltd.

Carey, W.B. (1998). Temperament and behavior problems in the classroom. *School Psychology Review, 27*, 522–533.

Carey, W.B. (2000). *The Carey Temperament Scales.* Scottsdale, AZ: Behavioral–Developmental Initiatives.

Carey, W.B., & McDevitt, S.C. (1978). Revision of the Infant Temperament Questionnaire. *Pediatrics, 16*, 735–739.

Carey, W.B., & McDevitt, S.C. (Eds.). (1994). *Prevention and early intervention: Individual differences as risk factors for the mental health of children.* New York: Brunner/Mazel.

Carey, W.B., & McDevitt, S.C. (1995). *Coping with children's temperament.* New York: Basic Books.

Carey, W.B. (with Jablow, M.M.). (1997). *Understanding your child's temperament.* New York: Macmillan.

Caspi, A. (1998). Personality development across the life course. In W. Damon (Ed.), *The handbook of child psychology* (pp. 311–375). New York: John Wiley & Sons.

Caspi, A., Henry, B., McGee, R.O., Moffitt, T.E., & Silva, P. (1995). Temperamental origins of child and adolescent behavior problems: From age three to age fifteen. *Child Development, 66,* 55–68.

Caspi, A., & Silva, P.A. (1995). Temperamental qualities at age three predict personality traits in young adulthood: Longitudinal evidence from a birth cohort. *Child Development, 66,* 486–498.

Chess, S. (1974). The influence of defect on development in congenital rubella. *Merrill-Palmer Quarterly, 20,* 255–275.

Chess, S., & Korn, S. (1970). Temperament and behavior disorders in mentally retarded children. *Archives of General Psychiatry, 23,* 122–130.

Chess, S., & Thomas, A. (1995). *The Adult Temperament Questionnaire.* Scottsdale, AZ: Behavioral-Development Initiatives.

Chess, S., & Thomas, A. (1999). Goodness of fit: Clinical applications from infancy through adult life. *Child Development, 66,* 486–498.

Conners, C.K. (1969). A teacher rating scale for use in drug studies with children. *American Journal of Psychiatry, 126,* 884–888.

deVries, M.W. (1989). Difficult temperament: A universal and culturally embedded concept. In W.B. Carey & S.C. McDevitt (Eds.). *Clinical and educational applications of temperament research* (pp. 81–85). Amsterdam/Lisse: Swets & Zeitlinger.

deVries, M.W. (1994). Kids in context: Temperament in cross-cultural perspective. In W.B. Carey & S.C. McDevitt (Eds.), *Prevention and early intervention: Individual differences as risk factors for the mental health of children* (pp. 126–139). New York: Brunner/Mazel.

DiLalla, L.F., & Jones, S. (2000). Genetic and environmental influences on temperament in preschoolers. In V.J. Molfese, & D.L. Molfese (Eds.), *Temperament and personality development across the life span* (pp. 33–55). Mahwah, NJ: Lawrence Erlbaum Associates.

Erickson, F. (1996). Inclusion into what? Thoughts on the construction of learning, identify, and affiliation in the general education classroom. In D.L. Speece & B.K. Keogh (Eds.), *Research on classroom ecologies: Implications for inclusion of children with learning disabilities* (pp. 91–105). Mahwah, NJ: Lawrence Erlbaum Associates.

Evertson, C.M., & Green, J.L. (1986). Observation as inquiry and method. In M.C. Wittrock (Ed.), *Handbook of research on teaching* (3rd ed., pp. 162–213). New York: Macmillan.

Fergusson, D.M., & Horwood, L.J. (1987). The trait and method components of ratings of conduct disorders, Part I. Maternal and teacher evaluations of conduct disorder in young children. *Journal of Child Psychology and Psychiatry, 28,* 249–260.

Forness, S.R., Kavale, K.A., & Walker, H.M. (1999). Identifying children at risk for antisocial behavior: The case for comorbidity. In R. Gallimore, L.P. Bernheimer, D.L. Macmillan, D.L. Speece, & S. Vaughn (Eds.), *Developmental perspectives on children with high-incidence disabilities* (pp. 135–157). Mahwah, NJ: Lawrence Erlbaum Associates.

Fox, N.A., Henderson, H.A., Rubin, K.H., Calkins, S.D., & Schmidt, L.A. (2001). Continuity and discontinuity of behavioral inhibition and exuberance: Psychophysical and behavioral influences across the first four years of life. *Child Development, 72,* 1–21.

Fullard, W., McDevitt, S.C., & Carey, W.B. (1984). Assessing temperament in one- to three-year old children. *Journal of Pediatric Psychology, 9,* 205–217.

Gagnon, C., Vitaro, F., & Tremblay, R.E. (1992). Parent–teacher agreement on kindergartners' behavior problems: A research note. *Journal of Child Psychology and Psychiatry, 33,* 1255–1261.

Garmezy, N., Masten, A., & Tellegen, A. (1984). The study of stress and competence on children: A building block for developmental psychopathology. *Child Development, 55,* 97–111.

Garrison, W.T., Biggs, D., & Williams, K. (1990). Temperament characteristics and clinical outcomes in young children with diabetes mellitus. *Journal of Child Psychology and Psychiatry, 31,* 1079–1088.

Goldberg, S., & Marcovitch, S. (1989). Temperament in developmentally delayed children. In G.A. Kohnstamm, J.E. Bates, & M.K. Rothbart (Eds.), *Temperament in childhood* (pp. 387–403). Chichester, England: John Wiley & Sons, Ltd.

Goldsmith, H.H. (1987). Roundtable: What is temperament? Four approaches. *Child Development, 58,* 505–529.

Goldsmith, H.H., Lemeny, K.S., Aksan, N., & Buss, K.A. (2000). Temperament substrates of personality development. In V.J. Molfese & D.L. Molfese (Eds.), *Temperament and personality development across the life span* (pp. 1–32). Mahwah, NJ: Lawrence Erlbaum Associates.

Goodman, K., Warsaw, D., Zukin, B., Tyler, B., & Shick, L. (1995). *Temperament talk. A guide to understanding your child.* LaGrande, OR: Center for Human Development.

Gordon, E.M., & Thomas, A. (1967). Children's behavioral style and the teacher's appraisal of their intelligence. *Journal of School Psychology, 5,* 292–300.

Gottesman, I.I. (1963). Genetic aspects of intelligent behavior. In N. Ellis (Ed.), *Handbook of mental deficiency: Psychological theory and research* (pp. 253–296). New York: McGraw-Hill.

Greenwood, C.R. (1996). Research on the practices and behaviors of effective teachers at the Juniper Gardens Children's Project: Implications for the education of diverse learners. In D.L. Speece & B.K. Keogh (Eds.), *Research on classroom ecologies: Implications for inclusion of children with learning disabilities* (pp. 39–67). Mahwah, NJ: Lawrence Erlbaum Associates.

Guerin, D.W., & Gottfried, A.W. (1994). Developmental stability and change in parent reports of temperament: A ten-year longitudinal investigation from infancy through preadolescence. *Merrill-Palmer Quarterly, 40*, 334–355.

Guerin, D.W., Gottfried, A.W., Oliver, P.H., & Thomas, C.W. (1994). Temperament and school functioning during early adolescence. *Journal of Early Adolescence, 14*, 200–225.

Guerin, D.W., Gottfried, A.W., & Thomas, C.W. (1997). Difficult temperament and behavior problems: A longitudinal study from 1.5 to 12 years. *International Journal of Behavioral Development, 21*, 71–90.

Gunn, P., & Berry, P. (1985). The temperament of Down's syndrome toddlers and their siblings. *Journal of Child Psychology and Psychiatry, 26*, 973–979.

Halverson, C.F., Kohnstamm, G.A., & Martin, R.P. (1994). *The developing structure of temperament from infancy to adulthood.* Mahwah, NJ: Lawrence Erlbaum Associates.

Hegvik, R.L., McDevitt, S.C., & Carey, W.B. (1982). The Middle Child Temperament Questionnaire. *Journal of Developmental and Behavioral Pediatrics, 3*, 197–200. Available from www.b-di.com or call 1-800-405-2313.

Henderson, H.A., & Fox, N.A. (1998). Inhibited and uninhibited children: Challenges in school settings. *School Psychology Review, 27*, 492–505.

Hertzig, M.E., Birch, H.G., Thomas, A., &. Mendez, O.A. (1968). Class and ethnic differences in the responsiveness of preschool children to cognitive demands. *Monographs of the Society for Research in Child Development, 33*, 1–69.

Kagan, J., Reznick, S., & Gibbons, J. (1989). Inhibited and uninhibited types of children. *Child Development, 60*, 838–845.

Keogh, B.K. (1982). Children's temperament and teachers' decisions. In R. Porter & G.M. Collins (Eds.), *Temperamental differences in infants and young children* (pp. 269–285). London: Pitman Books Ltd (CIBA Foundation Symposium 89).

Keogh, B.K. (1983). Individual differences in temperament: A contribution to the personal, social, and educational competence of learning disabled children. In J.D. McKinney & L. Feagens (Eds.), *Current topics in learning disabilities* (pp. 34–35). Norwood, NJ: Ablex.

Keogh, B.K. (1989). Applying temperament research to school. In G.A. Kohnstamm, J.E. Bates, & M.K. Rothbart (Eds.), *Temperament in childhood* (pp. 437–450). Chichester, England: John Wiley & Sons, Ltd.

Keogh, B.K. (1994). Temperament and teachers' views of teachability. In W.B. Carey & S.C. McDevitt (Eds.), *Prevention and early intervention. Individual differences as risk factors for the mental health of children* (pp. 246–256). New York: Brunner/Mazel.

Keogh, B.K. (1998). Perspective: Classrooms as well as students deserve study. *Remedial and Special Education, 19,* 313–314.

Keogh, B.K., Bernheimer, L.P., & Guthrie, D.G. (1997). Stability and change over time in cognitive level of children with delays. *American Journal on Mental Retardation, 101,* 365–372.

Keogh, B.K., Bernheimer, L.P., Haney, M., & Daley, S. (1989). Behavior and adjustment problems of young developmentally delayed children. *European Journal of Special Needs Education, 4,* 79–90.

Keogh, B.K., & Bess, C.R. (1991). Assessing temperament. In H. Lee Swanson (Ed.), *Handbook on the assessment of learning disabilities: Theory, research, practice* (pp. 313–330). Austin, TX: PRO-ED.

Keogh, B.K., & Burstein, N.D. (1988). Relationship of temperament to preschoolers' interactions with peers and teachers. *Exceptional Children, 54,* 69–73.

Keogh, B.K., Pullis, M.E., & Cadwell, J. (1982). A short form of the Teacher Temperament Questionnaire. *Journal of Educational Measurement, 19,* 323–329.

Keogh, B.K., & Speece, D.L. (1996). Learning disabilities within the context of school. In D.L. Speece & B.K. Keogh (Eds.), *Research on classroom ecologies: Implications for inclusion of children with learning disabilities.* Mahwah, NJ: Lawrence Erlbaum Associates.

Keogh, B.K., Yoshioka-Maxwell, B., Cadwell, J., Wilcoxen, A., & Wright, B. (1982). Children's temperament and teachers' decisions. *REACH Report.* Los Angeles: Graduate School of Education, University of California, Los Angeles.

Kohnstamm, G.A., Bates, J.E., & Rothbart, M.K. (Eds.). (1989). *Temperament in childhood.* Chichester, England: John Wiley & Sons, Ltd.

Kornblau, B.W. (1982). The teachable pupil survey: A technique for assessing teachers' perceptions of pupil attributes. *Psychology in the Schools, 19,* 170–174.

Kornblau, B.W., & Keogh, B.K. (1980). Teachers' perceptions and educational decisions. *New Directions for Teaching and Learning, 1,* 87–101.

Kurcinka, M.S. (1998). *Raising your spirited child.* New York: Harper Perennial.

Lerner, R.M., Palermo, M., Spiro, A., III, & Nesselroade, J.R. (1982). Assessing the dimensions of temperamental individuality across the life span: The Dimensions of Temperament Survey (DOTS). *Child Development, 53,* 149–159.

Lewis, M., & Feiring, C. (1998). *Families, risk, and competence.* Mahwah, NJ: Lawrence Erlbaum Associates.

Marcovitch, S., Goldberg, S., MacGregor, D., & Lojkasek, M. (1986). Patterns of temperament variation in three groups of developmentally delayed preschool children: Mother and father ratings. *Developmental and Behavioral Pediatrics, 7,* 247–252.

Martin, R.P. (1988). *The Temperament Assessment Battery for Children.* Brandon, VT: The Clinical Psychology Publishing Co.

Martin, R.P. (1989). Activity level, distractibility, and persistence: Critical characteristics in early schooling. In G.A. Kohnstamm, J.E. Bates, & M.K. Rothbart (Eds.), *Temperament in childhood* (pp. 451–462). Chichester, England. John Wiley & Sons, Ltd.

Martin, R.P. (1989). Temperament and education: Implications for underachievement and learning disabilities. In W.B. Carey & S.C. McDevitt (Eds), *Clinical and educational applications of temperament research* (pp. 37–51). Amsterdam/Lisse: Swets & Zeitlinger.

Martin, R.P. (1992). Child temperament effects on special education: Process and outcomes. *Exceptionality, 3,* 99–115.

Martin, R.P., & Bridger, R.C. (1999). *The Temperament Assessment Battery for Children–Revised.* Athens: University of Georgia.

Martin, R.P., & Holbrook, J. (1985). Relationship of temperament characteristics to the academic achievement of first-grade children. *Journal of Psychoeducational Assessment, 3,* 131–140.

Martin, R.P., Nagle, R., & Paget, K. (1983). Relationships between temperament and classroom behavior, teacher attitudes, and academic achievement. *Journal of Psychoeducational Assessment, 1,* 377–386.

Martin, R.P., Olejnik, S., & Gaddis, L. (1994). Is temperament an important contributor to schooling outcomes in elementary school? Modeling effects of temperament and scholastic ability on academic achievement. In W.B. Carey & S.C. McDevitt (Eds.), *Prevention and early intervention. Individual differences as risk factors for the mental health of children* (pp. 59–68). New York: Brunner/Mazel.

Matheny, A.P., Jr. (1989). Temperament and cognition: Relations between temperament and mental test scores. In G.A. Kohnstamm, J.E. Bates, & M.K. Rothbart (Eds.), *Temperament in childhood* (pp. 263–282). Chichester, England: John Wiley & Sons, Ltd.

Maziade, M. (1989a). Child temperament as an epidemiological concept. In W.B. Carey & S.C. McDevitt (Eds.), *Clinical and educational applications of temperament research* (pp. 175–186). Amsterdam/Lisse: Swets & Zeitlinger.

Maziade, M. (1989b). Should adverse temperament matter to the clinician? An empirically based answer. In G.A. Kohnstamm, J.E. Bates, & M.K. Rothbart (Eds.), *Temperament in childhood* (pp. 421–436). Chichester, England: John Wiley & Sons, Ltd.

Maziade, M. (1994). Temperament research and practical implications for clinicians. In W.B. Carey & S.C. McDevitt (Eds.), *Prevention and early intervention. Individual differences as risk factors for the mental health of children* (pp. 69–80). New York: Brunner/Mazel.

Maziade, M., Coté, R., Boutin, P., Bernier, H., & Thivierge, J. (1987). Temperament and intellectual development: A longitudinal study from infancy to four years. *American Journal of Psychiatry, 144,* 144–150.

Maziade, M., Coté, R., Boutin, P., Boudreault, M.D., & Thivierge, J. (1986). The effect of temperament on longitudinal academic achievement in primary school. *Journal of the American Academy of Child Psychiatry, 25,* 602–696.

McClowry, S.G. (1995). The development of the School-Age Temperament Inventory (SATI). *Merrill-Palmer Quarterly, 41,* 271–285.

McClowry, S.G. (1998). The science and art of using temperament as the basis for intervention. *School Psychology Review, 27,* 551–563.

McClowry, S.G. (2002). Transforming temperament profile statistics into puppets and other visual media. *Journal of Pediatric Nursing, 17,* 11–17.

McDevitt, S.C., & Carey, W.B. (1978). The measurement of temperament in 3- to 7-year-old children. *Journal of Child Psychology and Psychiatry and Allied Disciplines, 19,* 245–253.

Melville, N. (1995). Children's temperament: Intervention for parents. *Journal of Pediatric Nursing, 10,* 152–159.

Molfese, V.J., & Molfese, D.L. (Eds.). (2000). *Temperament and personality development across the life span.* Mahwah, NJ: Lawrence Erlbaum Associates.

Plumet, J.M., & Schwebel, D.D. (1997). Social and temperamental influences on children's overestimation of their physical abilities: Links to accidental injuries. *Journal of Experimental Child Psychology, 67,* 317–337.

Prior, M. (1992). Childhood temperament. *Journal of Child Psychology and Psychiatry, 33,* 249–279.

Prior, M., Garino, E., Sanson, A., & Oberklaid, F. (1987). Ethnic influences on "difficult" temperament and behavioural problems in infants. *Australian Journal of Psychology, 39,* 163–171.

Prior, M.R., Glazner, J., Sanson, A., & Debelle, G. (1988). Research note: Temperament and behavioral adjustment in hearing impaired children. *Journal of Child Psychology and Psychiatry, 29,* 209–216.

Prior, M., Sanson, A., Smart, D., & Oberklaid, F. (1999). Psychological disorders and their correlates in an Australian community sample of preadolescent children. *Journal of Child Psychology and Psychiatry, 40,* 563–580.

Prior, M., Sanson, A., Smart, D., & Oberklaid, F. (2000). *Pathways from infancy to adolescence. The Australian Temperament Project 1983–2000.* Melbourne: Australian Institute of Family Studies, v–83.

Pullis, M.E. (1979). *An investigation of the relationship between children's temperament and school adjustment.* Unpublished doctoral dissertation, University of California, Los Angeles.

Pullis, M.E. (1985). LD students' temperament characteristics and their impact on decisions by resource and mainstream teachers. *Learning Disability Quarterly, 8,* 109–122.

Pullis, M.E. (1989). Goodness of fit in classroom relationships. In W.B. Carey & S.C. McDevitt (Eds.), *Clinical and educational applications of temperament research* (pp. 117–120). Amsterdam/Lisse: Swets & Zeitlinger.

Pullis, M.E., & Cadwell, J. (1982). The influence of children's temperament on teachers' decision strategies. *American Educational Research Journal, 19,* 165–181.

Ratekin, C. (1990). *Temperament in children with Down syndrome.* Unpublished doctoral dissertation, University of California, Los Angeles.

Rosen, D.L., Cameron, J., & Rice, D. (1996). A temperament program: A children's preventive mental health program. *HMO Practice, 10,* 140–142.

Rosenthal, R., & Jacobson, L. (1968). *Pygmalion in the classroom: Teachers expectations and pupils' intellectual development.* New York: Holt, Rinehart & Winston.

Rothbart, M.K. (1989). Biological processes in temperament. In G.A. Kohnstamm, J.E. Bates, & M.K. Rothbart (Eds.), *Temperament in childhood* (pp. 77–110). Chichester, England: John Wiley & Sons, Ltd.

Rothbart, M.K., Ahadi, S.A., & Hershey, K.L. (1994). Temperament and social behavior in childhood. *Merrill-Palmer Quarterly, 40,* 21–39.

Rothbart, M.K., & Bates, J.E. (1998). Temperament. In W. Damon (Ed.), *The handbook of child psychology* (pp. 105–165). New York: John Wiley & Sons.

Rothbart, M.K., Derryberry, D., & Posner, M.I. (1994). A psychobiological approach to the development of temperament. In J.E. Bates & T.D. Wachs (Eds.), *Temperament: Individual differences at the interface of biology and behavior* (pp. 83–116). Washington, DC: American Psychological Association.

Rothbart, M.K., & Jones, L.B. (1998). Temperament, self-regulation, and education. *School Psychology Review, 27*, 479–491.

Rowe, D.C., & Plomin, R. (1977). Temperament in early childhood. *Journal of Personality Assessment, 41*, 150–156.

Rutter, M. (1989). Temperament: Conceptual issues and clinical implications. In G.A. Kohnstamm, J.E. Bates, & M.K. Rothbart (Eds.), *Temperament in childhood* (pp. 463–479). Chichester, England: John Wiley & Sons, Ltd.

Rutter, M., Tizard, J., & Whitmore, K. (Eds.). (1970). *Education, health and behavior.* London: Longman.

Sameroff, A.J., Bartko, W.T., Baldwin, A., Baldwin, C., & Seifer, R. (1998). Family and social influences on the development of child competence. In M. Lewis & C. Feiring (Eds.), *Families, risk, and competence* (pp. 161–186). Mahwah, NJ: Lawrence Erlbaum Associates.

Sanson, A.V., Smart, D.F., Prior, M., Oberklaid, F., & Pedlow, R. (1994). The structure of temperament from age 3 to 7 years: Age, sex, and sociodemographic influences. *Merrill-Palmer Quarterly, 40*, 233–252.

Saudino, K.J., McGuire, G., Reiss, D., Hetherington, E.M., & Plomin, R. (1995). Parent ratings of EAS temperaments in twins, full siblings, half siblings, and step siblings. *Journal of Personality and Social Psychology, 68*, 723–733.

Scarr, S. (1981). Testing for children. *American Psychologist, 36*, 1159–1166.

Sheeber, L.B., & Johnson, J.H. (1994). Evaluation of a temperament-focused, parent-training program. *Journal of Clinical Child Psychology, 23*, 249–259.

Sheldon, W.H. (1942). *The varieties of temperament: A psychology of constitutional differences.* New York: Harper & Row.

Silberman, M. (1969). Behavior expressions of teachers' attitudes toward elementary school students. *Journal of Educational Psychology, 60*, 402–407.

Silva, P.A. (1990).The Dunedin multidisciplinary health and developmental study: A fifteen-year longitudinal study. *Pediatric and Perinatal Epidemiology, 4*, 96–127.

Smith, J., & Prior, M. (1995). Temperament and stress resilience in school-age children: A within-families study. *Journal of the American Academy of Child and Adolescent Psychiatry, 34*, 168–179.

Stipek, D. (1998). Communicating expectations. In D. Stipek (Ed.), *Motivation to learn: From theory to practice* (pp. 203–220). Needham Heights, MA: Allyn & Bacon.

Strelau, J. (2001). The role of temperament as a moderator of stress. In T.D. Wachs & G.A. Kohnstamm (Eds.), *Temperament in context* (pp. 153–172). Mahwah, NJ: Lawrence Erlbaum Associates.

Super, C.M., & Harkness, S. (1994). Temperament and the developmental niche. In G.A. Kohnstamm, J.E. Bates, & M.K. Rothbart (Eds.), *Temperament in childhood* (pp. 115–125). Chichester, England: John Wiley & Sons.

Swanson, J.M. (1992). *School-based assessments and interventions for ADD students.* Irvine, CA: K.C. Publishing.

Teglasi, H. (1998). Temperament constructs and measures. *School Psychology Review, 27,* 564–585.

Teglasi, H., & MacMahon, B.H. (1990). Temperament and common problem behaviors of children. *Journal of Applied Developmental Psychology, 11,* 331–349.

Tharp, R.G., & Gallimore, R. (1988). *Rousing minds to life. Teaching, learning, and schooling in social context.* Cambridge, United Kingdom: Cambridge University Press.

Thomas, A., & Chess, S. (1977). *Temperament and development.* New York: Brunner/Mazel.

Thomas, A., Chess, S., & Birch, H.G. (1968). *Temperament and behavior disorders in children.* New York: New York University Press.

Turecki, S. with Tonner, L. (2000). *The difficult child* (2nd ed.). New York: Bantam Books.

U.S. Department of Education. (1998). *Twentieth annual report to Congress on the implementation of the Individuals with Disabilities Act.* Washington, DC: Author.

Varni, J., Rubenfeld, B.A., Talbot, D., & Setoguchi, Y. (1989). Family functioning, temperament, and psychological adaptation in children with congenital or acquired limb deficiencies. *Pediatrics, 84,* 823–830.

Wachs, T.D., & Kohnstam, G.A. (Eds.). (2001). *Temperament in context.* Mahwah, NJ: Lawrence Erlbaum Associates.

Wallander, J.L., & Varni, J.W. (1998). Effects of pediatric chronic physical disorders on child and family adjustment. *Journal of Child Psychology and Psychiatry, 39,* 29–46.

Weiner, B. (1992). *Human motivation: Metaphors, theories, and emotion.* Beverly Hills: Sage Publications.

Weisz, J.R., Chaiyasit, W., Weiss, B., Eastman, K.L., & Jackson, E.W. (1995). A multimethod study of problem behavior among Thai and American children in school: Teacher reports versus direct observations. *Child Development, 66*(2), 402–415.

Weisz, J.R., Suwanlert, S., Chaiyasit, W., Weiss, B., Achenbach, T.M., & Walter, B.R. (1987). Epidemiology of behavioral and emotional problems among Thai and American children: Parent reports for ages 6–11. *Journal of the American Academy of Child and Adolescent Psychiatry, 26,* 890–897.

Werner, E.E., & Smith, R. (1992). *Overcoming the odds. High risk children from birth to adulthood.* Ithaca, NY: Cornell University Press.

Werner, E.E., & Smith, R.S. (2001). *Journeys from childhood to midlife. Risk, resilience, and recovery.* Ithaca, NY: Cornell University Press.

Wertlieb, D., Weigel, C., Springer, T., & Feldstein, M. (1987). Temperament as a moderator of children's stressful experiences. *American Journal of Orthopsychiatry, 57,* 234–245.

Wilson, B.J. (1999). Entry behavior and emotion regulation abilities of developmentally delayed boys. *Child Development, 35,* 214–222.

Windle, M., & Lerner, R.M. (1986). Reassessing the dimensions of temperament individuality across the life span: The revised dimensions of Temperament Survey (DOTS–R). *Journal of Adolescent Research, 1,* 213–230.

RECOMMENDED READINGS

Carey, W.B. (1997). *Understanding your child's temperament.* New York: Macmillan.

Carey, W.B. (1998). Temperament and behavior problems in the classroom. *School Psychology Review, 27,* 522–533.

Carey, W.B., & McDevitt, S.C. (Eds.). (1989). *Clinical and educational applications of temperament research.* Amsterdam/Lisse: Swets & Zeitlinger.

Carey, W.B., & McDevitt, S.C. (Eds.). (1994). *Prevention and early intervention. Individual differences as risk factors for the mental health of children.* New York: Brunner/Mazel.

Carey, W.B., & McDevitt, S.C. (1995). *Coping with children's temperament.* New York: Basic Books.

Chess, S., & Thomas, A. (1996). *Know your child.* New York: Macmillan.

Chess, S., & Thomas, A. (1999). *Goodness of fit: Clinical applications from infancy through adult life.* New York: Brunner/Mazel.

Goodman, K., Warsaw, D., Zukin, B., Tyler, B., & Shick, L. (1995). *Temperament talk. A guide to understanding your child.* LaGrande, OR: Center for Human Development.

Greenspan, S., & Salmon, J. (1998). *The challenging child.* Cambridge, MA: Perseus Books.

Halverson, C.F., Kohnstamm, G.A., & Martin, R.P. (1994). *The developing structure of temperament and personality from infancy to adulthood.* Mahwah, NJ: Lawrence Erlbaum Associates.

Kagan, J. (1994). *Galen's prophecy: Temperament in human nature.* New York: Basic Books.

Kohnstamm, G.A., Bates, J.E., & Rothbart, M.K. (Eds.). (1989). *Temperament in childhood.* Chichester, England: John Wiley & Sons, Ltd.

Kurcinka, M.S. (1998). *Raising your spirited child.* New York: Harper Perennial.

Molfese, V.J., & Molfese, D.L. (2000). *Temperament and personality development across the life span.* Mahwah, NJ: Lawrence Erlbaum Associates.

Prior, M., Sanson, A., Smart, D., & Oberklaid, F. (2000). *Pathways from infancy to adolescence. The Australian Temperament Project 1983–2000.* Melbourne: Australian Institute of Family Studies.

Thomas, A., & Chess, S. (1977). *Temperament and development.* New York: Brunner/Mazel.

Thomas, A., Chess, S., & Birch, H. G. (1968). *Temperament and behavior disorders in children.* New York University Press.

Turecki, S., with Tonner, L. (2000). *The difficult child* (2nd ed.). New York: Bantam Books.

Wachs, T.D., & Kohnstamm, G.A. (Eds.). (2001). *Temperament in context.* Mahwah, NJ: Lawrence Erlbaum Associates.

Werner, E.E., & Smith, R. (1992). *Overcoming the odds: High risk children from birth to adulthood.* London: Cornell University Press.

Werner, E.E., & Smith, R.S. (2001). *Journeys from childhood to midlife. Risk, resilience, and recovery.* Ithaca, NY: Cornell University Press.

Appendices

Longitudinal Studies of Temperament

The New York Longitudinal Study

The New York Longitudinal Study (NYLS) (Thomas & Chess, 1977) was one of the first major longitudinal studies of temperament and the first of many studies by these investigators and their colleagues. The goals were

> a) The development of a method for classifying behavioral individuality in early infancy in terms of objectively describable and reliably rated categories of temperament, b) The study of consistencies and inconsistencies of these early characteristics in the course of development, c) The analysis of the pertinence of early temperament to later psychological individuality, d) The dynamic of temperament in the mastery of environmental demands and expectations at succeeding age–stage levels of development, e) The identification of those children who develop behavior disorders, and the analysis of the ontogenesis and course of these disorders in terms of a continuously evolving child-environment interactional process. (p. 15)

The sample of infants in the NYLS was gathered over a 6-year period in the 1950s. The 131 children and the 85 families were of middle or upper-middle socioeconomic (SES) status, and the parents as a group were highly educated. More than half of the fathers and 40% of the mothers had both college and post-graduate degrees, and more than 90% had attended college. Most of the families lived in urban areas, primarily New York City. Information about the children in infancy was obtained from interviews with the parents, most first interviews conducted when the infants were 2–3 months old. Researchers conducted follow-ups of the children through the school years, gathering data from behavior observations, reports from parents and teachers, and psychometric tests. Academic progress and achievement scores were obtained from school records. Subsequent follow-ups in adolescence and adulthood were based on separate interviews with the individuals themselves and with their parents. Throughout the study, clinical evaluations were conducted if signs of behavior or adjustment problems were present. The relationships of children's temperament to behavior disorders, developmental deviations, school functioning, and parent–child interactions were among topics investigated. Psychiatrists Thomas and Chess have followed their original sample into adulthood, and their "children" are now in their forties and fifties. The vast majority of participants remained in the sample over the years. The size of the NYLS study sample is relatively small, but a great deal is known about the participants, and the findings provide rich insights into temperament and development and adjustment over time.

The Dunedin Multidisciplinary Health and Developmental Study

The Dunedin Multidisciplinary Health and Developmental Study (Silva, 1990) began in 1972 in New Zealand. The original longitudinal sample included 1,037 children (527 boys and 510 girls) born in the city of Dunedin between April 1, 1972, and March 31, 1973. Dunedin is a city of more than 110,000 people on the South Island of New Zealand. The SES is somewhat higher than that of the country as a whole and the sample contained relatively few Maori or Pacific Island children. The goals of the research included, but were not limited to, study of the following:

The health and normal development of children and adolescents; the nature, prevalence, and long-term significance of developmental disorders and health problems; the influences and events likely to contribute to developmental disorders and health problems; ... and ... to develop or improve techniques for the identification of children with developmental disorders and health problems with a view to prevention. (p. 79)

Perinatal information was gathered in the first months, and beginning at age 3 the children were reassessed every 2 years with psychological, medical, and sociological measures that included information about development, education, and behavior and temperament. The children and adolescents were seen individually for half or full days at the research unit, and parents completed questionnaires describing their status. Teachers also provided information at one follow-up stage. Temperament or behavioral style was assessed using a series of rating scales based on observations of the children's behavior during the follow-up visits. Throughout the years, participation has remained high and dropout rates have been low (e.g., at age 5 years, 991 [96%] children were still in the sample; at age 15 years, 976 [94%] were still in the sample). The findings from this ongoing study, thus, are based on a large and stable sample. The large number of reports and publications from this multidisciplinary research address medical, dental, psychological, psychiatric, audiological, educational, and sociological perspectives on children and adolescents.

Australian Temperament Project

The Australian Temperament Project (Prior, Sanson, & Oberklaid, 1989; 2000) is a major prospective longitudinal study that began in 1980. The original sample was enrolled in 1983 and consisted of 2,443 infants ages 4–8 months (1,270 males and 1,173 females) who were randomly selected from Maternal and Child Health Centers in the Australian state of Victoria. Consistent with the urban/rural balance in the state at the time the project was initiated, approximately two thirds of the families and children were from urban areas, one third from rural areas. Overall, the sample was representative of population sociodemographics. The goals of the project included documenting the expression and stability of temperament, delineating and understanding the contributions of temperament to children's development and adjustment, understanding social, ethnic, and family influences on temperament and behavior, and identifying indicators of risk for later outcomes. Important questions over the years have specifically addressed the role of temperament in children's emotional and behavioral adjustment, in their social and behavioral competence, and in their progress in school. The long-term nature of the study has allowed description of developmental paths from infancy into adolescence. The project was planned with the Thomas and Chess (1977) temperament model as background, and considerable effort was directed initially at developing adequate and feasible measurement techniques for Australian infants and children. Subgroups of the total sample were followed up at approximately 18-month periods, and response rates have been about 80% at the various data collection stages.

Follow-up consisted primarily of mailed questionnaires to parents addressing children's temperament, health, social behavior, behavior problems, family stress, and so forth. When the children were older, teachers rated them on readiness for school, adaptation to school, reading competence, and social behavior. In the adolescent period, the questions were expanded to include ratings of personality, behavior and emotional problems, substance abuse, peer relationships, school adjustment, and social responsibility and civic-mindedness. Gender, social class, and ethnicity effects have been documented, and significant relationships between temperament patterns and behavior problems identified. In sum, this large and well-implemented longitudinal study has provided information about measurement, the structure and stability of temperament at different ages, and relationships between temperament and a range of personal and social outcomes. The project is ongoing.

Appendix B: Scales and Questionnaires for Assessing Temperament

Tool/instrument	Age range	General description
Adult Temperament Questionnaire (ATQ) Chess & Thomas (1995)	18–40 years	This questionnaire consists of 54 items assessing the nine dimensions of temperament they developed, including: 1) activity level, 2) rhythmicity, 3) approach or withdrawal, 4) adaptability, 5) threshold of responsiveness, 6) intensity of reaction, 7) distractibility, 8) attention span and persistence, and 9) mood.
Behavioral Style Questionnaire (BSQ) McDevitt & Carey (1978)	3–7 years	Scores represent the nine temperament traits described by Thomas and Chess (1977) in the New York Longitudinal Study (NYLS). Child's scores place him or her into one of five categories: easy, low intermediate, slow to warm up, high intermediate, or difficult.
Carey Temperament Scales (CTS) Carey (2000) EITQ RITQ TTS BSQ MCTQ (see individual listings)	Infancy–12 years	The CTS are based on the Thomas and Chess dimensions of temperament and were designed to gather information from parents. The questionnaires cover a wide age range and tap typical age-appropriate behaviors. See separate listings.
The Children's Behavior Questionnaire (CBQ) Rothbart, Ahadi, & Hershey (1994)	3–8 years	The CBQ is for parents and is made up of 15 subscales that assess temperament.
The Colorado Childhood Temperament Inventory (CCTI) Rowe & Plomin (1977)		The CCTI taps the same components as the Emotionality, Activity, Sociability Inventory (EAS) (see this table) but, in addition, assesses sootheability, attention span, and reaction to food.
Dimensions of Temperament Survey (DOTS) Lerner, Palermo, Spiro, & Nesselroade (1982)	Early childhood to young adulthood	Based on Thomas and Chess's nine dimensions, DOTS includes four forms: one for parents to assess their child, one for parents to assess themselves, one for teachers, and one for a self-report from the child. The temperament dimensions covered are activity level, attention span or distractibility, adaptability or approach/withdrawal, rhythmicity, and reactivity. Each dimension is assessed across age levels with changes in wording as appropriate.

(continued)

Scales and Questionnaires for Assessing Temperament (continued)

Tool/instrument	Age range	General description
Dimensions of Temperament Survey–Revised (DOTS-R) Windle & Lerner (1986)	Childhood to young adulthood	Developed to assess age-continuous aspects of temperament. Based on a series of statistical analyses, the form is designed for use by parents, teachers, and a self-report form for children. Like the DOTS, the DOTS-R is based on the temperament model of Thomas and Chess. It is useful for self-reports as well as for describing others on age-continuous aspects of temperament. The DOTS-R is a useful questionnaire with good psychometric properties.
Early Infancy Temperament Questionnaire (EITQ) Medoff-Cooper, Carey, & McDevitt (1993)	1–4 months	Similar in design to others in the Carey Temperament Scales Series. Consists of 76 items.
Emotionality, Activity, Sociability Inventory (EAS) Buss & Plomin (1975)	Children and adolescents	Three forms of the EAS scale are available for use by parents and teachers as well as for children and adolescents to assess themselves. Each scale consists of 20 items tapping the three temperament factors of Emotionality, Activity, and Sociability.
The Middle Childhood Temperament Questionnaire (MCTQ) Hegvik, McDevitt, & Carey (1982)	8–12 years	Covering the age range across childhood, the MCTQ consists of 99 parent report items. Each questionnaire contains items that describe children on each of the nine Thomas and Chess temperament dimensions. The dimension scores allow development of an individual temperament profile. Global or general impressions on each temperament category as well as a rating of overall difficulty are also gathered. Software programs for scoring are now available. The scales are designed for use by parents, but they provide information about behavioral styles that can help "fill out" school professionals' understanding of a child.

Parent and Teacher Temperament Questionnaires (PTQ) Thomas & Chess (1977)	3–7 years, but have been used frequently with older elementary school children	The PTQ was designed to provide a systematic way of describing children on each of the nine temperament dimensions as described by Thomas and Chess (1977). The scales were developed as part of the New York Longitudinal Study (NYLS). Items were designed to tap how children behave in different situations in everyday life. Two forms of the scales are available: the parent scale (PTQ) and the teacher scale (TTQ), which does not include the dimension of rhythmicity. In both forms, the rater is asked to rate how typical a specific behavior is for the child in question using a scale from 1 (hardly ever) to 7 (almost always).
Parent and Teacher Temperament Questionnaires–Short Form (PTQ and TTQ short forms) Keogh, Pullis, and Cadwell (1982)	Pre-school and elementary school	The PTQ and TTQ Short Forms use the Thomas and Chess scales but are abbreviated measurement tools, making them easier to use for both research and educational purposes. Both scales contain 23 items using statistical factor analytic techniques. The TTQ yields three factors: 1) Task Orientation, made up of Persistence, Distractibility, and Activity Level; 2) Approach–Withdrawal and Positive Mood; and 3) Reactivity, which is a negative factor composed of the dimensions of Intensity, Threshold of Response, and Negative Mood. Similar analyses of the parent form of the original Thomas and Chess scale also yielded a 23-item scale to measure the factors of Flexibility, Intensity, and Mood. In both questionnaires, each item is rated on a scale of 1 (hardly ever) to 6 (almost always). The final score for each factor is the average of the ratings for each item in the factor.
Revised Infant Temperament Questionnaire (RITQ) Carey & McDevitt (1978)	Infants	The RITQ consists of 95 items referenced to infant behaviors.
School-Age Temperament Inventory (SATI) McClowry (1995)	8–11 years	The SATI is a parent report scale composed of 38 items directed at four aspects of temperament: task persistence, approach-withdrawal, negative reactivity, and energy. The components are reminiscent of the Thomas and Chess dimensions but organized somewhat differently. The items cover a range of behavior relevant to both home and school. Examples include "Gets very frustrated," "Has difficulty completing assignments," "Bashful when meeting new children" and "Runs to where he/she wants to go." The SATI has robust correlations with Martin and Bridger's Temperament Assessment Battery for Children-Revised (TABC-R), described in this appendix, even though the scales were developed for different age groups.

(continued)

Scales and Questionnaires for Assessing Temperament *(continued)*

Tool/instrument	Age range	General description
Temperament Assessment Battery for Children (TABC) Martin (1988)	3–7 years	The TABC consists of three scales, one for parents, one for teachers, and one for clinicians (e.g., school psychologists, social workers, medical personnel). The parent and teacher scales contain 48 similar items relevant to home or school and the clinician form consists of 24 items. The items address six temperament dimensions: activity, adaptability, approach/withdrawal, emotional intensity, distractibility, and persistence. These temperament dimensions are consistent with but not identical to the temperament model of Thomas and Chess.
Temperament Assessment Battery for Children-Revised (TABC-R) Martin & Bridger (1999)	2–7 years	The TABC-R consists of a parent form (37 items) and a teacher form (29 items). Items assess the temperament characteristics (referred to as *traits* by Martin and Bridger) of inhibition, negative emotionality, activity level, and lack of task persistence. A score for *impulsivity* may be derived from the scores on the last three scales. Based on their empirical work with the TABC-R, the authors have identified six temperamental types: Inhibited, Highly Emotional, Impulsive, Typical, Reticent, and Uninhibited. The teacher form contains an additional type: Passive.

Both the TABC and the TABC-R batteries are noteworthy for the careful psychometric work in their development and validation. The manuals for both contain detailed reports of validity and reliability, normative data, and item analysis data along with instructions for administering and scoring the scales. |
| Temperament and Atypical Behavior Scales (TABS) Bagnato, Neisworth, Salvia, & Hunt (1999) | 11–71 months | TABS is specifically designed to identify critical temperament and self-regulations problems that can indicate a child's risk for developmental delay as early as possible. A screening and assessment tool, TABS has been normed on nearly 1,000 children with both typical and atypical development. Parents can complete a 15-item, single-sheet form in 5 minutes. If problems are indicated, they may use the more detailed TABS Assessment Tool, which provides an evaluation of atypical behavior in four categories: 1) detached, 2) hypersensitive-active, 3) underreactive, and 4) dysregulated. A TABS Manual provides all of the information necessary for administering and scoring TABS. An intervention guide offers strategies for minimizing problematic, atypical behavior. |
| Toddler Temperament Scale (TTS) Fullard, McDevitt, & Carey (1984) | 1–3 years | The TTS is a 100-item parent report scale useful for assessing behavioral styles of children. |

Publications and Programs on Temperament for Teachers and Parents

PUBLICATIONS

Understanding Your Child's Temperament

Understanding Your Child's Temperament (Carey, 1997) is a useful book for parents because it addresses many of the practical, everyday situations that occur in family life. Pediatrician William Carey's extensive clinical experience working with children and parents and his insights and suggestions, along with the contributions of Martha Jablow, enrich this book and make it especially relevant reading. Temperament is defined using the framework of the Thomas and Chess nine dimensions. Content addresses many aspects of development and potential problems covering a wide age range—infancy through adolescence—for example, sleeping and eating problems in infancy and behavior problems in the elementary school years. The book contains concrete examples and case studies that illustrate management techniques and ways to respond to individual differences in children's temperaments, especially those characteristics that parents often view as difficult. The final chapter addresses frequently asked questions about temperament, for example, "The day care teachers say my boy is aggressive. Is this his temperament or is it a behavioral problem? "Aren't adaptable children smarter?" and "Do drugs change temperament?" The emphasis throughout the book is on how sensitivity to and understanding of individual characteristics of temperament can help parents work effectively with their children.

The Difficult Child, 2nd Edition

In their book, *The Difficult Child, 2nd Edition,* Turecki and Tonner (2000) described a program for parents of difficult children based on Dr. Turecki's experience as a psychiatrist. A basic assumption is stated simply and directly: "If you can learn to understand your child's difficult temperament, you can begin to correct what is going on with him and with your family" (p. 105). Note that Turecki and Tonner emphasized what is going on *with* the child, not *in* the child. This is good advice for teachers when they are thinking about how to solve problems in the classroom. Turecki and Tonner's program is aimed at changing parents' thinking and reactions and includes elements that are relevant to school, such as evaluation and definition of the problem and management techniques. Parents are encouraged to develop a behavioral profile of their child by making a list of the types of problems and specific behaviors that they find troublesome. Parents are also encouraged to identify the situations in which problem behaviors occur and to develop a behavioral profile of their child that links behaviors and situations. This allows parents to make up a list of important behaviors relative to the child's temperament. Linking behavior and temperament provides parents with direction for developing procedures and routines that take into account individual differences in behavioral styles and thus can reduce stress in family life.

Raising Your Spirited Child

Many of the suggestions by Turecki and Tonner are consistent with those of Kurcinka, whose book *Raising Your Spirited Child* (1998) includes descriptions of the temperament characteristics of spirited children and many suggestions for specific ways for parents to work with such children. For example, "Keep your message simple"; "Limit the number of instructions"; "Avoid asking questions if there really isn't a choice"; and "Tell him what he can do" (1998, p. 136). Kurcinka emphasized the effects of child and parent temperament matches or mismatches, and parents are encouraged to consider their own temperament profiles relative to that of their child.

The approaches described by Carey and Jablow (1995), Turecki and Tonner (2000) and Kurcinka (1998) can also be useful in school. Listing the behaviors that are problems and the situations in which they occur can help teachers identify and anticipate trouble spots. Differentiating those behaviors that are truly problematic from those that are relatively minor also helps educators set priorities and make decisions about intervention. Should the child be referred for psychological assessment or can the behavior be improved by changing the routines in the classroom? Finally, recognizing that some problem behaviors are related to temperament lowers the level of negativity that adults often feel when they think the misbehavior is purposeful and deliberate.

PROGRAMS

The Parent Temperament Program

The Parent Temperament Program in LaGrande, Oregon, also based on the Thomas and Chess formulation of temperament, teaches positive parenting techniques, especially those targeted at "challenging" children. The program provides information through "Temperament Talk" (Goodman, Warsaw, Zukin, Tyler,

& Shick, 1995), a comprehensive and readable publication for parents. Content includes discussion of temperament, family stressors, goodness of fit, management strategies, and many specific tips for parents.

INSIGHTS

McClowry (2002) has developed and implemented a temperament-based program for inner-city children, their parents, and their teachers. Called INSIGHTS, the program for first- and second-grade children is carried out in classrooms using a variety of techniques, including puppets. The children act out stories using puppets that represent different temperament types: Fredrico the Friendly, Coretta the Cautious, Hilary the Hard Worker, and Gregory the Grumpy. The stories present different scenarios and dilemmas that the children solve by using the puppets to interact with others in small groups. Children are helped to understand their own temperaments, and the content is designed to teach them ". . . skills in handling daily stressors and enhancing interpersonal relationships" (McClowry, personal communication, 2001). In this program, parents and teachers attend small group sessions in which they discuss information and ideas about child development and about improving the goodness of fit with their child or student.

Other Programs

Other programs for parents include one developed by Sheeber and Johnson (1994) aimed at difficult preschoolers; another program by Rosen, Cameron, and Rice (1996) focused on infants; and the Temperament Intervention for Parents (TIPS) (Melville, 1995).

Index

INDEX

Page numbers followed by *f* indicate figures; those followed by *t* indicate tables.

Achievement
  characteristics identified as
      important to, 63–66
  contribution of temperament on
      direct effects, 69–73
      indirect effects, 73–76
  correlation to teacher grades, 66
  in early childhood, 64
  in older children, 65

Acting out
  as a dimension of externalizing, 95
  as a disruption of classroom
      routines, 93
  link to environment, 39
  and physical abuse of peers, 99
Active and intense-responding
      children
  intervening with, 153–155
  strategies for self-direction, 157
Activity level
  and achievement in reading and
      math, 64, 66*t*
  as a component of temperament,
      17, 19
  correlation to grades and
      standardized test scores, 67*t*
  defined, 14*t*
  factor as defined by researchers, 20*t*
  influence in classroom learning, 63
  low, as protective or risk factor, 43
  relationship to agreeableness or
      extroversion, 55
Adaptability
  and achievement, 69–70
  correlation to grades and
      standardized tests, 64, 67*t*
  defined, 14*t*
  and ratings of teachability, 86
ADHD, *see* Attention-deficit/
      hyperactivity disorder
Adolescents, and school functioning,
      65–66
Aggression
  as dimension of externalizing, 95
  effect of stressful environment on,
      101

Agreeableness, 55
Anger, proneness to, 99
Anxiety, 95
Approach factor
  consistency of, 58
  defined, 18
  high, 43
Approach/withdrawal
  correlation to grades and
      standardized test scores, 67*t*
  defined, 14*t*
  see also Negative approach, and
      internalization of problems
Argumentative children, 59
Assessment of temperament
  approaches to
      informal, 137
      interviews, 126, 127–128
      laboratory studies, 129
      observations, 126, 128–134
      rating scales and questionnaires,
          126, 134–147, 183*t*–187*t*
  of students
      differences in findings of,
          137–138
      focus of, 125–126
      global generalization of
          impressions, 138
      objectivity of, 126–127
  of teachers, 138–140
Attachment
  effect on teachers' attitudes and
      behaviors toward students,
      82–83
Attention
  effortful control concept, 72–73
  span, defined, 14*t*
  to task, 72–73
Attention deficits, *see* Attention-
      deficit/hyperactivity disorder
      (ADHD)
Attention-deficit/hyperactivity
      disorder (ADHD)
  and activity level, 118
  causes of, 117
  and classroom context, 119–120
  confusion with temperament
      characteristics, 118–120

Attention-deficit/hyperactivity
    disorder (ADHD)—*continued*
  consistency and ongoing behaviors
    of, 118
  diagnosis and misdiagnosis of,
    117–119
  "excessive" behavior and, 118
  and individualized education
    program (IEP), 120
Australian Temperament Project, 7,
    17–18, 112, 181
Autism spectrum disorder, 98

Behavior
  studies, 95–96, 96–97, 97*t*, 99*t*
  and temperament constellations,
    98–99
  see also Attention-deficit/
    hyperactivity disorder
    (ADHD); Ethnic/cultural
    influences; School-appropriate
    behaviors
Behavior management, teachers'
    views of, 94–95
Behavior problems
  as coping strategies, 105–106
  overview of, 95–96
  relationship to temperament, 97–102
  specific to situations, 94
  teachers' views of, 102–103
  temperament characteristics
    associated with, 100*t*
  see also Disruptive behaviors;
    Distractibility
Behavioral consistency, and
    observations, 133
Biological aspect of temperament, *see*
    Temperament, genetic
    components of

Caregivers
  behaviors seen as problematic by,
    99–100, 101–102
  descriptions of infants/young
    children by, 48
Chess, S., *see* Thomas and Chess
Children
  effect of teachers' expectations on,
    81

impact of social reinforcement on
    self-view, 73–74
  impact of temperament in
    classroom, 81–82
  perception of environment, 72
  quick-to-respond, 3
  teachers' perceptions and
    expectations of, 78–81
  types of, *see* Temperament, types,
    as identified by researchers
Chronic conditions in children,
    and maladaptive outcomes,
    111–112
Classroom
  behavior expectations in, 70–71
  children's temperaments, impact
    on
  management of, 24–25, 90
    disruptions and, 32–33, 93–95
    ethnic/cultural influences in,
    35–36
    personal styles of children in,
    37–38
  teachers' views on task
    orientation and, 68–69
Cognitive abilities of students
  modifying curriculum for, 109
  effect on ratings of teachability,
    86
Cognitive motivational behaviors, 85,
    87*t*
  see also Teachers
Conduct disorders, 94
  see also Behavior problems
Confident children
  assessment of, 71
  as temperament type, 23, 24*t*
Conscientiousness, 54
  similarity to self-regulation/task
    orientation, 55
Context
  goodness of fit and, 31
  importance of considering
    children's, 70
Continuity
  assessment of, 58–59
  cumulative, 74, 75, 105–106
Curriculum
  and goodness of fit, 32
  modifying for children with
    cognitive limitations, 109

Depression, as dimension of internalizing, 95
Development
causes of delays in, 115
temperament continuity over periods of, 57–59
Developmental quotient (DQ), relationship to temperament, 52
Difficult children, 105
relationship to aggression, 101
strategies for working with, 154t
Difficult temperament
defined, 21, 24t
protective and risk factors of, 42–43
Difficultness, see Difficult children; Difficult temperament
Disabilities, children with
developmental delays, research studies of, 116–117
family adjustment to, 111–112
influence of temperament on, 120–122
hearing impairments, 109
limitations of, 120–121
research studies of, 110, 112
response to school environment, 113–114
and risk for psychosocial maladjustment, 111
sense of self in, 121–122
similarity of temperament types to children without disabilities, 110–111
teacher–child interaction with, 121
see also specific disabilities
Disabled children, see Disabilities, children with
Disruptive behaviors, as dimension of externalizing, 95
Distractibility, 67t
and achievement in reading and math, 64
correlation to grades and standardized test scores, 67t
defined, 14t
influence on classroom learning, 63
Down syndrome, 116–117
temperaments and children with, 52
see also Disabilities, children with

DQ, see Developmental quotient
Dunedin Longitudinal Study (New Zealand), 7, 18–19, 180–181

Easy, as temperament type, 21, 24t
EEG (electroencephalogram) patterns and exuberance, 49
Effortful control, see Attention
Electroencephalogram, see EEG patterns and exuberance
Electrophysiological methods in exuberant and inhibited children, 129
Emotional, highly, as temperament type, 23, 24t
Emotional stability, similarity to mood/intensity of reactions, 55
Emotionality, 15
Ethnic/cultural influences, 34–36
Experience
effect of temperament on, 29–31
and impact on temperament, 50–51
Externalizing problems, defined, 95
Extreme conduct disorders, 98
Extroversion, similarity to approach/withdrawal, 55

Gender
differences of, in temperament expression, 18
and goodness of fit, 38
Gifted children, temperaments of, 52
"Good citizenship," 102–103
Goodness of fit
and characteristics of classrooms, 144
and characteristics of teachers, 85, 145–146
and classroom environments, 31–39, 70–71
as model to avoid misdiagnosing attention-deficit/hyperactivity disorder (ADHD), 119–120
student temperaments and, 143–144
and views of teachability, 89
Grades, influence of temperament on, 66–69

High persistence, and achievement in reading and math, 64
Home, effects on child temperament, 75f
Hyperactivity, see Attention-deficit/hyperactivity disorder (ADHD)

IEP, see Individualized education program
Illness and medical care, response of children with disabilities to, 113
Impulsive, as temperament type, 23, 24t
Indifference by teachers, 82–83
Indirect effects on achievement, 73–74, 76
Individualized education program (IEP), 120
Infants/young children, research studies of, 47–49
see also Temperament, genetic components of
Inflexibility, 17
Inhibited, as temperament type, 23, 24t
Inhibition
and achievement, 70
relationship to neuroticism, 55
see also Internalization, of behavior
Instructional program and attention-deficit/hyperactivity disorder (ADHD), 119–120
Intelligence, and temperament, 51–54
Intelligence quotient (IQ), relationship to temperament, 52
Interactive behavior problems, 106
Internalization
of behavior, 103–104
defined, 95
of problems, 95
Interventions
as strategy for anticipating and intervening with students, 152t
see Temperament, interventions related to; Temperament, programs related to

IQ, see Intelligence quotient

Joylessness/apathy, 99

"Know thyself"
as strategy for anticipating and intervening with students, 152t
see also Goodness of fit, and characteristics of teachers

Lack of control, 18, 100–101
LD, see Learning disabilities, children with
Learning
characteristics that influence, see Activity; Distractibility; Persistence
direct effects of temperament on, 69–73
Learning disabilities (LD), children with
assessments of, 109
impact of temperament on, 63–66
task orientation in, 114

Measures of temperament, early, as predictive of later achievement, 68
Mental retardation and temperament, 115
Mood, defined, 14t

Negative affect, relationship to neuroticism, 55
Negative approach, and internalization of problems, 101
Negative family influences, 28
Neuroticism, 54
relationship to negative affect and mood/intensity of reactions, 55
New York Longitudinal Study (NYLS), 6–7
definition of temperament, 12–13
described, 179–180

ethnicity/cultural influences on study results, 34–35
Nutrition and growth disorders, 39
NYLS, *see* New York Longitudinal Study

Observations
    and consistency of behavior, 132–133
    focused, 131–132, 133–134
    informal, 131
Openness/intellect, 54
Oppositional/aggressive behavior, 99

Persistence, 17, 19, 63–64, 67*t*, 68
    and achievement, 69–70
    defined, 14*t*
    influence in classroom learning, 63–64
    correlation to grades and standardized test scores, 64, 67*t*
Personality
    identifiers of, 54
    and temperament, 54–55
        similar dimensions of, 55*t*
Personal–social behaviors, 87*t*
Personal–social flexibility, 17
Physical disability, modifications for, 109
Poorness of fit, 101–102
Positive affect, 55
Positive family influences, 28
Problems, anticipation of
    with behavior, *see* Behavior problems
    as strategy for intervening with students, 152*t*
Protective factors, and influences of temperament, 41–43
Psychosocial maladjustment, risk in children with disabilities, 111

Questionnaires, *see* Assessment of temperament; Rating scales/questionnaires
Quick-to-respond children, 3

Rating scales/questionnaires
    and inconsistency of children's behaviors, 134–135
    potential errors in, 134
    scales based on other models of temperament, 136–137
    scales based on the Thomas and Chess Model of Temperament, 135–136
    see also Assessment of temperament
Reactivity, 17
Reading and math achievement, impact of temperament on, 64
Regularity, *see* Rhythmicity
Rejection by teachers, 82–83
    see also Teachers
Research studies
    of children with disabilities, 110, 112
    of infants/young children, 47–49
    of teachers, 78–81, 82–85
Resilience, 44–45
Resistance to control, 101
Resistant factors, for children with chronic conditions, 112
Reticent, as temperament type, 23, 24*t*
Retardation, *see* Down Syndrome; Mental retardation and temperament
Rhythmicity, 14*t*, 17
Risk factors
    in children's environments, 43
    and influences of temperament, 39–40

School
    effects of, on child temperament, 75*f*
    experience of, contributing factors to, 2
School psychologists, temperament assessment of students by, 128
School-appropriate behaviors, 85–86, 87*t*
Self-direction, low, as problem behavior, 99
Self-reproach, 99
Shy, as temperament type, 24*t*

Shyness, 51, 58
Sleep problems, 39
Slow to warm up
    children who are
        intervening with, 153–155
        strategies for working with,
            155*t*, 157
    as temperament type, 21, 24*t*
Sluggishness, as temperament type,
    18, 20*t*, 23, 24*t*, 100
Sociability, 15, 17, 19
Social reticence, 57
Stability, *see* Continuity
Standardized tests, 66–67
Stimulation, and difficult children,
    42
Stress, in children with disabilities,
    121–122
Student behavior, viewing from an
    interactionist perspective, 151
Student self-understanding of
    temperament, 156–158
Student withdrawal, 90
Surveys, *see* Assessment of
    temperament; Rating scales/
    questionnaires; Research
    studies

Tantrums, 59
Task orientation, 17
    influence on teachers' decisions, 84
    and relationship to performance in
        school, 65, 68, 83
    see also Activity level;
        Distractibility; Persistence
Teachability
    effect on teacher–student
        interactions, 85–89
    teacher-rated characteristics of, 87*t*
Teachers
    accuracy of grading, 67
    assessments of students, 66–67
    attention to students in the
        classroom, 86
    attitudes toward students, 82–85
    concern for students, 82–83
    as decision makers, 77–78
    developing profiles of children,
        19–20

expectations for high or low
    achievers, 80
gender bias of, 84, 88
goodness of fit and characteristics
    of, 145–146
impact of temperament on
    decisions of, 83–84
influence of student characteristics
    on, 79–80
interactions with children with
    disabilities, 121
perceptions and expectations of
    children, 78–81
rating of intelligence in children
    by, 84
responses to temperament, 23–24
socioeconomic bias, 84
special education bias in, 88
teaching styles, 33–36
temperament assessment of,
    138–140
views of behavior and behavior
    problems, 96–97, 97*t*, 102–103
views of characteristics of
    teachable pupils, 87*t*
views of temperament, 68
Temperament
    assessment of, *see* Assessment of
        temperament; Rating
        scales/questionnaires
    Australian Temperament Project,
        17–18
    awareness of, 146–148
    broadening the basis of
        assessment, 150–151
    categories and definitions, by
        Thomas and Chess, 14*t*
    classroom strategies for, 150
    consistency over time, 56–57
    constellations of, 98–99
    continuity and, 57–59
    contribution to achievement of
        children, 69–76
    defined, 3–4, 12–16, 15
    dimensions and factors of, 16–20
    distinction from behavioral
        maladjustment, 104
    Dunedin Longitudinal Study (New
        Zealand), 7, 18–19
    factors affecting, 17, 20*t*

genetic components of, 47–51
influence of adjustment and behavior in children with disabilities, 120–122
lens, importance of viewing student behavior through, 151
New York Longitudinal Study (NYLS), 12–13
personalization of, 157–158
planning and implementation of, 151–152
primary components of, 19, 20*t*
for problems, 153
reframing into temperament terms, 149–150
profiles, using temperament types to develop, 19–20
programs related to, 148, 189–190
relationship to behavior problems, 97–102, 106
relationship to curriculum, 65
situational consistency, 56
stability of, 56–59
teachers' attitudes toward, 142–143
teachers' preferences of traits, 30–31
types, as identified by researchers, 20
  confident, 23, 24*t*
  easy, 21, 24*t*
  difficult, 21, 24*t*
  highly emotional, 23, 24*t*
  impulsive, 23, 24*t*
  inhibited, 23, 24*t*
  reticent, 24, 24*t*
  slow to warm up, 21–22, 24*t*
  sluggish, 23, 24*t*
  typical, 24, 24*t*
  undercontrolled, 22, 24*t*
  uninhibited, 24, 24*t*
  well-adjusted, 23–24, 24*t*
uniqueness of, 15–16
use of precise language in, 149
see also Activity level; Adaptability; Approach/withdrawal; Distractibility; Mood, defined; Persistence; Rhythmicity; Threshold of responsiveness
see also specific temperament types

Temperament characteristics
  behavior problems associated with, 100*t*
  and predisposition to behavior problems, 98
Temperament-related problems, intervening in, 153
Temperamental self-regulation, 41
  see also Persistence
Thomas, A., *see* Thomas and Chess
Thomas and Chess
  New York Longitudinal Study (NYLS), 12–16
  stylistic aspects of temperament, 12–13
  temperament categories and definitions, 14*t*, 24*t*
Threshold of responsiveness, 17
  defined, 14*t*
Time
  relationship to temperament, 56–57
Time samples, as observational method to record behaviors, 129–30
Tourette syndrome, 98
Twin studies, 50
Typical, as temperament type, 23, 24*t*

Unadaptability, 101
Undercontrolled
  children who are, 71
  as temperament type, 22, 24*t*
Unfamiliarity, children's response to, 49
Unhappiness, 95
Uninhibited, as temperament type, 23, 24*t*
Unsociability, 101

Well-adjusted, as temperament type, 23, 24*t*
Withdrawal, 93, 95
Work habits, good, 102–103

"Zones of tolerance," *see* Goodness of fit, and teacher characteristics